RISE ABOVE

How to rise above the problems of the illusory world through the Lessons of

A Course in Miracles

Raveena Nash

RP

www.totalrecallpress.com

TotalRecall Publications, Inc.
1103 Middlecreek
Friendswood, Texas 77546
281-992-3131   281-482-5390 Fax
www.totalrecallpress.com

ISBN: 978-1-59095-108-8
UPC: 6-43977-41085-6
Printed in the United States of America with simultaneously printings in Australia, Canada, and United Kingdom.
FIRST EDITION
1   2   3   4   5   6   7   8   9   10

"The resurrection is the complete triumph of Christ over the ego, not by attack but by transcendence. For Christ does rise above the ego and all its works, and ascends to the Father and His Kingdom." T207.

Table of Contents

PREFACE

The teachings of *A Course in Miracles (ACIM)* are essentially simple and straightforward. It is the practice of the Course that is not always easy. This is partly because the ego has created so many things in its illusory world which keep us mesmerized, distracted and in bondage. If we could detach a little from these things, and desire them less, then perhaps we would stand a better chance of awakening. As the sages of the Far East have been telling us for so long, we need to practice detachment, dispassion and wise discrimination—three concepts endorsed by Alice Bailey, the prolific writer on mysticism.

There are three lessons from the Workbook of *ACIM* which tie in with these three concepts: Lesson 132, *"I loose the world from all I thought it was"* (detachment); Lesson 128, *"The world I see holds nothing that I want"* (dispassion); and Lesson 133, *"I will not value what is valueless"* (discrimination).

As we shall see later on, many other lessons from the Workbook can be applied to other concepts and situations, but the best way to begin the Course is to follow the instructions given by Jesus and practice the Workbook lessons one a day for 365 days. That is the very first step that has to be taken in the study of the Course. The next step, which could take place simultaneously, is the reading of the Text. This should be done carefully and at a slow pace. A few years later it may be beneficial to go through the Workbook once again, and the Text definitely has to be read over and over again. This is important because each time one reads it one learns something that one had overlooked before. This could be because one has grown in consciousness and is now ready to understand the teachings at a deeper level. One should bear in mind the Text contains a huge amount of information in its 669 pages. As I pore over these pages again and again, I often wish I had a photographic memory so that I could absorb everything immediately, without have to keep re-reading it.

Although going through the Workbook lessons on a daily basis and studying the Text are essential, the practical application of the teachings of the Course in situations that crop up in our daily lives is vital. Certain lessons can be used in everyday life to help keep our minds on track, i.e., to ensure that our thoughts are right-minded (under the guidance of the Holy Spirit) and not wrong-minded (under the guidance of the ego).

I often find myself using specific lessons for certain feelings and situations that seem to occur quite frequently in my life. So I thought it would be useful to match these lessons to the situations in a clear-cut manner, and set them out in this book. As most people will experience similar situations and emotions in their daily lives, they may find it useful to carry this book around with them, so they can use the relevant lessons when needed. A complete list of all situations and the relevant lessons is given in the appendix.

Changing our perception of the illusory world is not easy and requires constant practice and vigilance. It is my hope that this book will be a tool to help in this regard.

Raveena Nash

Spring 2012

"NOW LET A NEW PERCEPTION
COME TO ME."[1]

---

[1] *A Course in Miracles (ACIM)*, Workbook (W) Lesson 313, p. 457, Foundation for Inner Peace, California, 2007.

CHAPTER 1

ANNOYANCE RELATED TO THE PAST

We often think about the past; we think about the pleasant things and good times we have experienced as well as unpleasant situations or people or challenging events that we have gone through. This is not a sensible thing to do but the ego puts up quite a battle in its attempt to keep us stuck in the past. The Course tells us that it is guilt that keeps the past alive because the ego actually believes that the separation from God took place, and that it deserves punishment because of this. Time is compared to as a *long carpet* going from the past to the future and, *"...As long as you believe the Son of God is guilty you will walk along this carpet, believing that it leads to death..."*[2] Furthermore, the ego actually wants to hold onto guilt because, as we read on the same page, *"....Without guilt the ego has no life, and God's Son is without guilt."* And on the following page it is explained that, *"...Guilt, then, is a way of holding past and future in your mind to ensure the ego's continuity. For if what has been will be punished, the ego's continuity is guaranteed..."*

So, reminiscing about the past is an ego tactic, which should be avoided if possible. One of the best lessons to keep us focused on the present is Lesson 8, *"My mind is preoccupied with past thoughts."* When we say this we will realize that it is a rather silly thing to do because it is pointless. Whilst thinking about the past the mind is blank, according to *ACIM*, since the past does not exist. This means we are not really thinking about anything. Not only is it pointless to dwell on the past, but it is a major impediment to awakening because, *"....While thoughtless ideas preoccupy your mind, the truth is blocked."*[3]

Another relevant *ACIM* lesson is Lesson 289, *"The past is over. It can touch me not."* What is gone is gone, and it should be remembered

---

[2] *A Course in Miracles (ACIM)*, Text (T) p. 237.
[3] *ACIM*, W13.

that it never really happened in the first place; all that took place, whether good or bad, took place in the ego's dream world. The problem of living in this world is that it precludes us from living in the "*real world*", which is our goal, as the real world can be considered to be the last stop before Heaven. *"Unless the past is over in my mind, the real world must escape my sight. For I am really looking nowhere; seeing but what is not there. How can I then perceive the world forgiveness offers?"*[4]

The real world is a world of beauty where everything has been forgiven. Attaining the real world is a sign that we have awoken from the ego's dream of sin and guilt. Before we can hope to reach the real world, we have to really accept the fact that our world is an illusion. With reference to our world the Course informs us: *"....All that you need to give this world away in glad exchange for what you did not make is willingness to learn the one you made is false."*[5]

Then we need to practice forgiveness because, *"The real world is attained simply by the complete forgiveness of the old, the world you see without forgiveness....For forgiveness literally transforms vision, and lets you see the real world reaching quietly and gently across chaos, removing all illusions that had twisted your perception and fixed it on the past..."*[6]

So when thoughts from the past flit across the mind remember, *"My mind is preoccupied with past thoughts."* And then remember, *"The past is over. It can touch me not."*

---

[4] *ACIM*, W442.
[5] *ACIM*, T254.
[6] *ACIM*, T353.

CHAPTER 2

SEEING CONFLICT ON THE TV NEWS

Television brings conflict and chaos into our living rooms on a daily basis. Whilst one may still feel the need to know what is going on in the dream world, one can end up feeling quite upset if one watches a complete TV news bulletin from start to finish; there are so many distressing things happening in the world. Violence between people of different races or different religions is one example. If we could only realize that there is no difference at all between us, despite our diverse religions or different races and political allegiances, maybe we would be able to live together in peace. We are all one appearing to be nearly seven billion. So, in reality there is no difference between one religion and another; between one race and another; and between one political ideology and another. They are all simply illusions that we take very seriously in our collective dream, set up by the ego way back in time when it decided to try to split away from God.

It's not only news bulletins that are disturbing; many of the documentaries and films that we watch for pleasure are equally bad. *Blood Alley, Hellfighter* and *Death Race* were the titles of three films broadcast, one after the other, by a TV channel on a Sunday recently. Just the titles were enough to put one off. The media seems to have an obsession with violence and death.

When we observe all the strange things goings on in our world, we try to make sense out of them. But is that possible? When, for example, a taxi driver went on the rampage in the Lake District and killed 12 people before turning the gun on himself, all we could ask was, "Why did he do it?" The police, the media and his friends and neighbors could not understand his bizarre and unpredictable behavior. They were trying to determine the cause of his senseless acts of violence. But this was simply a very extreme case of ego projection. He was a very unhappy man who had financial problems that were worrying him so much that he went berserk. His ego decided to project these problems onto others, thereby making him the victim, in his mind (his ego mind or lower mind).

In instances like this it helps if we repeat Lesson 12 of *A Course in Miracles*: *"I am upset because I see a meaningless world."* The lesson goes on to explain, *"...You think that what upsets you is a frightening world, or a sad world, or a violent world, or an insane world. All these attributes are given it by you. The world is meaningless in itself."*

When you really take on board the message of *ACIM,* after having completed the Workbook and studied the Text, and when you continue to use the lessons of the Workbook thereafter on a daily basis, you will realize that the world *is* meaningless. The ego would like to keep us trapped in this illusory world, alternating forever between pleasure and pain, lifetime after lifetime. Nothing could be more meaningless than that.

"God did not create a meaningless world", states Lesson 14, and it explains why our world is meaningless. God did not create it; the ego did. And the ego is nothing but the creation or miscreation of the wrong mind or lower mind at the time of the separation from God. The only good thing about this *"tiny, mad idea"* of separation is that it was only an idea, a mental projection, which, in reality, never occurred. But still, whilst we believe we are egos with bodies, we will have to find a way of rising above all the trials and tribulations of the world of form. Using the lessons of *A Course in Miracles* is one way of doing that.

It can be quite disheartening looking around us and realizing that it is all meaningless. But this can be overcome by learning and applying Lesson 21: *"I am determined to see things differently."* This puts us in a position of power, and is a warning to the ego. When one tells the ego that one is determined to see things differently, it is the same as saying to it, "Watch out, I am not going to be at your mercy forever. I will make my escape from your meaningless world." Jesus tells us that we can use Lesson 21 when we feel slightly annoyed, angry or furious. It is applicable in all cases. It could also be used when we are upset or saddened by the images we see on our television screens.

Another good lesson to use when one is trying to make sense out of this world is Lesson 23: *"I can escape from the world I see by giving up attack thoughts."* This lesson tells us that everything in this world is a symbol of vengeance, but if we give up our own vengeful thoughts or *"attack thoughts"*, as they are referred to in the Course, we can overcome the world of the ego. It is pointless trying to change the world because it can't be done; what we *can* do is change ourselves, which really means changing our perception of things. Therefore, when something we learn about from a news bulletin makes us angry, the best thing we can do is to relinquish any feelings of anger and repeat Lesson 23.

The renowned Course teacher Kenneth Wapnick, in his book, *From Futility to Happiness*, explains that there will always be attack and violence in the world because of the belief in the ego's thought system of *"one or the other"*. He points out that the hidden cause of all violence is the mind's decision to be separate from God. But if we turn to Jesus instead of the ego, and use our right minds to rise above the battleground, we will be able to become, *"peaceful, content, and benignly indifferent."*

It may seem impossible to be *"benignly indifferent"* to the suffering that is all around us, but if we remember that it is taking place in the ego's dream world, then, with practice, one can become a little less agitated. As we read in Lesson 34: *"I could see peace instead of this."* Peace of mind can only be found if we go within; and peace can only extend outwards to the world, when we have obtained peace within. In this lesson we are told to repeat the following whenever our peace of mind is threatened: *"I could see peace in this situation instead of what I now see in it."* This really involves forgiveness—the essence of *ACIM*—because the only way to be peaceful in the midst of chaos and conflict is to realize that everything in our world is a mere mental projection, and does not really exist. When this realization has sunk in, we are able to forgive ourselves and others for having listened to the ego, which created the world and all its misery. Then we will be able to become peaceful.

However, even if we are able to be *"benignly indifferent"* to the tragedies that frequently strike our planet, that should not stop us from taking practical, tangible steps to alleviate suffering. So we should, of course, give financial aid or other assistance, if we can, to those who are in distress, and remember that they are part of us, as we are all one.

CHAPTER 3

FEELING ANGER TOWARDS SOMEONE OR SOMETHING

Anger is one of the most common sentiments on the planet. Every living person has, at one time or another, experienced this emotion, which stems from fear. Fear, in turn, stems from guilt due to the belief in the separation from Heaven.

A Course in Miracles does not tell us never to get angry but it does say that anger is never justified. This is because it makes the illusion real. We are simply reacting to figures in our collective dream, which doesn't make sense. In Chapter 30 of the Text it also says that forgiveness or pardon is always justified. *"...You do not forgive the unforgivable, nor overlook a real attack that calls for punishment...Instead, it* (salvation) *merely asks that you respond appropriately to what is not real by not perceiving what has not occurred."*[7] We are asked to ignore *what has not occurred.* This is not easy for the simple reason that when we get angry, we do seem, within the illusion, to have every right to respond with anger. The key is to remember that it is only an illusion and our goal is to rise above all the illusions of the world.

Lesson 22: *"What I see is a form of vengeance",* may serve as a reminder to wake up and learn the lesson involved in the situation. It may remind us that we feel the need to be angry or to defend ourselves because *we* have projected our anger onto the world. Jesus tells us that this becomes a vicious circle until we change our perception of whatever the situation is.

Lesson 23 follows on nicely from Lesson 22. *"I can escape from the world I see by giving up attack thoughts."* Feeling angry does not make one feel good about oneself. So it must come as a relief to realize that one doesn't have to be angry. *"...There is no point in lamenting the world. There is no point in trying to change the world. It*

---

[7] *ACIM*, T638.

is incapable of change because it is merely an effect. But there is indeed a point in changing your thoughts about the world. Here you are changing the cause. The effect will change automatically."[8]

This passage tells us clearly that the key to overcoming anger is in our own hands; if we change our minds about the world and realize that everything in it is a mental projection, then we will see that there is no point in getting worked up about the things people say or do. The obvious thing to do is to respond in a calm manner and shrug off upsetting incidents. The more we do so, the less likely we are to encounter circumstances or people who make us angry. In fact, the more one practices the Course, the less angry one becomes.

Another helpful lesson is Lesson 68: *"Love holds no grievances."* If we were right-minded all the time (and that is one of the goals of the Course) we would never get angry because all actions that emanate from the right mind are based on love. It is only because we have split minds and we follow the wrong mind portion, which listens to the ego, that we get upset and angry in the first place. When we are angry with someone and cannot forgive them, this is simply because we have forgotten who we really are; we are identifying with our self (ego) instead of our Self (God's Son). As the ego's thought system is based on fear and guilt and the projection of these onto others, there will always be situations that arouse anger in us as the projections return to haunt us.

The following affirmation, also from Lesson 68, is particularly helpful because serious Course students really do not want to betray their Selves: *"Love holds no grievances. Let me not betray my Self."* It is a very useful lesson to repeat whenever one is upset or angry.

What does one do if there is a neighbor or a colleague at work, for example, who seems to be angry and make hurtful comments? The first thing is to remember that anything like that is a call for help and is simply that person's ego projecting fear and guilt outwards. The way to respond to this is with love or, if that seems too difficult, at least with acceptance. Try to calm this person down and not get annoyed by his fear-based remarks. Remember also that he and you are one because there is only one of us. So we follow the advice of Jesus in

---

[8] *ACIM,* W34.

Lesson 68 and say to him (in one's mind): *"I would see you as my friend, that I may remember you are part of me and come to know myself."*

When we become aware that everyone is part of us we take great care not to hurt anyone. It is simply a matter of training one's mind to remember that we are all one.

CHAPTER 4

FEELING AGITATED, TROUBLED AND ANXIOUS

Anxiety is another very common feeling; we are anxious about work, about our health or the health of our loved ones, we are anxious about money and we may sometimes even be anxious about the weather. But where does this anxiety comes from? You've guessed it—the ego. Things like security, health, money and the weather only have an effect upon physical bodies and, as we know, the body is the creation of the ego.

*"When you are anxious, realize that anxiety comes from the capriciousness of the ego, and **know this need not be**. You can be as vigilant against the ego's dictates as for them."*[9] This passage asks us to be vigilant against the ego, which means monitoring all our thoughts, words and deeds to check whether they come from the ego mind or the right mind. When you spot an ego-based thought you can stop it in its tracks or you can speak to your ego and tell it that this is unacceptable. It's a matter of constantly chipping away at the ego; in the long run it should pay off.

On page 63 of the Text, we are told to observe our thoughts. *"Watch your mind for the temptations of the ego, and do not be deceived by it. It offers you nothing. When you have given up this voluntary dis-spiriting, you will see how your mind can focus and rise above fatigue and heal. Yet you are not sufficiently vigilant against the demands of the ego to disengage yourself. **This need not be**."* In other words, we *can* monitor our thoughts to make sure we rise above thoughts that come from the ego mind/wrong mind. But we don't do this very much, possibly because it is too much effort. However, Jesus stresses that we must do so.

Throughout *ACIM* we are urged, again and again, to be forgiving towards everyone, and never to judge anyone. But there is one

---

[9] *ACIM*, T63.

exception. We *are* asked to judge the ego. *"Watch your mind carefully for any beliefs that hinder its accomplishment, and step away from them. Judge how well you have done this by your own feelings, for this is the one right use of judgment. Judgment, like any other defense, can be used to attack or protect; to hurt or to heal. The ego* **should** *be brought to judgment and found wanting there. Without your own allegiance, protection and love, the ego cannot exist. Let it be judged truly and you must withdraw allegiance, protection and love from it."*[10] So here we find that the only thing we are ever supposed to judge is the ego, and also our own feelings when we watch the ego. If we observe an ego based thought and turn away from it mentally, i.e., refuse to entertain that thought, we will feel good about ourselves for having had the strength to do so. Thus, each time we feel anxious or troubled, we can try to put these thoughts out of our mind, knowing that they are ego-based.

One lesson that can help us do this is Lesson 48: *"There is nothing to fear."* If we remember that love and fear are the only two emotions that we can have, and fear comes from the ego, then this lesson should be of assistance. It is explained in Lesson 48 that whenever we are fearful we are trusting in our own strength instead of trusting in God's strength, which is in our right minds. We are urged to let the strength of God replace our weakness.

Lesson 74: *"There is no will but God's"* is another lesson that is designed to give us peace of mind. When we find ourselves worrying about one thing or another we could surrender the situation to God, knowing that there is no will but His. We are asked to turn specific problems over to God, in order to overcome our anxiety or fear. *"If there is one conflict area that seems particularly difficult to resolve, single it out for special consideration. Think about it briefly but very specifically, identify the particular person or persons and the situation or situations involved, and tell yourself: There is no will but God's. I share it with Him. My conflicts about _____ cannot be real."* This is a wonderful way of handing over perceived problems to God. Jesus tells us at the end of this lesson that if we have truly managed to obtain peace of mind through this exercise, we will feel joyful.

---

[10] *ACIM*, T64.

There is no will but God's because all ego-based thoughts are unreal for the simple fact that the ego itself is unreal, as are our physical bodies and the world in which we live. It *is* very difficult to accept this because everything we do centers around the body and the ego mind (lower mind). If we have just been diagnosed with a deadly disease, for instance, it *is* very frightening and upsetting. All we can do in such a situation is to surrender this huge problem to God. Fortunately, we can turn to *A Course in Miracles* and use its most valuable lessons to give us strength in moments of weakness and fear, and restore our peace of mind. *"There is no will but God's. I seek His peace today."*

Another lesson which could help us rise above our suffering is Lesson 193: *"All things are lessons God would have me learn."* This lesson teaches us that all distress can be overcome by forgiveness although this is not apparent to those who are still dreaming. If we forgive people and circumstances we will see things differently. Even though pain and suffering seem very real, Lesson 193 states that they are not. It is a lack of forgiveness and guilt in the mind which makes pain seem real and makes our dream seem real; if we forgive and awaken, pain will disappear. This, we are told, is the key to Heaven's gate. We just need to find the faith to truly believe, and the willingness to truly accept that all that we are experiencing in our lives are lessons we need to learn. If the pain is too much to bear the only thing we can do is call upon the Holy Spirit for guidance and strength, and hand the problem over to Him.

CHAPTER 5

FEELING WEAK AND VULNERABLE

We are at the mercy of the whims of fate, and we have no option but to deal bravely with whatever is dished out to us. We experience happy times and then, inevitably, things go wrong in one way or another or, at least, they change quite dramatically. A lovely child grows up to become an awkward teenager; a healthy bank balance can disappear overnight if we are suddenly made redundant; a sudden and debilitating disease can bring our active lifestyle to an abrupt halt; a fulfilling relationship can be destroyed in an instant by infidelity; an earthquake or tsunami can wreak havoc in a few minutes and destroy complete towns and everyone and everything in them—and for those who survive such a catastrophe, their whole way of life can change in an instant. Those are just a few examples of how life in the world of the ego can make us feel weak and vulnerable.

One of the reasons for this is the unpredictability of most, if not all, things. The reason for this unpredictability is that change is at the essence of all the "miscreations" of the ego. When the mind had a *"tiny, mad idea"* to become autonomous it created the ego which, in turn, created our physical bodies, the world, time and space. All of them are illusory since the tiny, mad idea was just that—an idea, with no tangible effects, as mentioned before. We are reminded frequently in the Course that ideas cannot leave their source (the mind); so they remain only ideas or thoughts and nothing else. Nonetheless, the ego actually believed that it succeeded in its quest for autonomy, and the result is this world where everything is impermanent.

The only way to overcome feelings of weakness and vulnerability is to rise above the ego's world altogether. Fortunately, ACIM has given us a number of useful lessons to help us with this. We could start with Lesson 47: *"God is the strength in which I trust."* It is made clear in this lesson that if we rely on the ego we cannot help but feel powerless. *"If you are trusting in your own strength, you have every reason to be apprehensive, anxious and fearful. What can you predict or control? What is there in you that can be counted on?"* There is nothing in our lives that is predictable or within our control, although we spend most of the time trying to make sure we can control events both in the present and in the future.

Jesus points out in Lesson 47 that we aren't aware of all the facets of any problem and we have no guarantees that we will find the right solutions to any problem. *"Who can put his faith in weakness and feel safe? Yet who can put his faith in strength and feel weak? God is your safety in every circumstance. His Voice speaks for Him in all situations and in every aspect of all situations, telling you exactly what to do to call upon His strength and His protection..."* In order to be able to hear God's Voice we have to forget our problems for a while and try to be still and quiet. But we can also repeat mentally to ourselves: *"God is the strength in which I trust"* if ever we feel vulnerable and fearful, as we go about our daily activities.

Although it appears there are many things in life that can threaten us, in fact, the Course repeatedly tells us that it is only our thoughts that do so. If, for example, one has to undergo a major operation the following day and one spends the whole night worrying about it, it is one's thoughts that are causing the anxiety, not the operation. Thousands and thousands of successful operations are performed every single day, in all parts of the world. So it is one's thoughts that are causing the fear, not the impending surgery.

We have seen that angry or fearful thoughts are referred to in ACIM as *"attack thoughts."* Lesson 26 states: *"My attack thoughts are attacking my invulnerability."* This lesson explains that we project our attack thoughts onto others and, as a result, we fear attack; this makes us feel vulnerable, but this is a false image of ourselves. *"...Nothing except your thoughts can attack you. Nothing except your thoughts can make you think you are vulnerable. And nothing except your thoughts can prove to you this is not so."* So we repeat Lesson 26 to remind ourselves that we are invulnerable.

If we identify with our physical bodies, we will always feel vulnerable, to a certain extent. The way to solve this problem is to try (and it's not easy) to identify with our true or real Self, which is spirit. No harm can befall the spirit, as it remains as it was when God created it—eternal, immortal, cherished and protected.

Lesson 153: *"In my defenselessness my safety lies"* can also be used to give us inner strength. The first paragraph in this lesson paints a really gloomy picture of our world. *"You who feel threatened by this changing world, its twists of fortune and its bitter jests, its brief relationships and all the 'gifts' it merely lends to take away again; attend this lesson well. The world provides no safety. It is rooted in attack, and all its 'gifts' of seeming safety are illusory deceptions. It attacks, and then attacks again. No peace of mind is possible where danger threatens thus."*

Jesus explains in this lesson that we become trapped in a circle of *"attack, defense; defense, attack"* because the threatening nature of the world makes us angry and fearful, so we project these qualities out into the world and then try to defend ourselves against them. He says that defensiveness *"attests to weakness"* and the only way to remain invulnerable is not to be defensive. *"Defenselessness is strength. It testifies to recognition of the Christ in you....We rise up strong in Christ, and let our weakness disappear, as we remember that His strength abides in us. We will remind ourselves that He remains beside us through the day, and never leaves our weakness unsupported by His strength. We call upon His strength each time we feel the threat of our defenses undermine our certainty of purpose. We will pause a moment, as He tells us, 'I am here.'"*

Many people experience loneliness especially when they grow older and find themselves living alone. This could be why so many people turn to pets for companionship. Cats and dogs give their human companions great love, loyalty and devotion. If we want to learn the true meaning of unconditional love, then our best teachers are our pets. However, if we remember God, then we shouldn't really feel lonely. As Lesson 41 reminds us, *"God goes with me wherever I go."* Jesus starts off this lesson with the following: *"Today's idea will eventually overcome completely the sense of loneliness and abandonment all the separated ones experience. Depression is an inevitable consequence of separation. So are anxiety, worry, a deep sense of helplessness, misery, suffering and intense fear of loss."* It is not surprising, then, that depression is a major health problem causing people to turn to tranquilizers for solace. Perhaps they should turn to God instead and remember, *"You can never be deprived of your perfect holiness because its Source goes with you wherever you go. You can never suffer because the Source of all joy goes with you wherever you go. You can never be alone because the Source of all life goes with you wherever you go. Nothing can destroy your peace of mind because God goes with you wherever you go."* It is sometimes difficult to remember this when we are suffering or going through challenging times, but we need to because it will give us inner strength.

So, whenever you feel unhappy, lonely, weak or vulnerable it would help greatly if you stopped, took a few deep breaths and recalled that God has not abandoned you and that Christ is by your side all the time. Turn within for a few moments and say: *"God goes with me wherever I go"*. Alternatively remind yourself that, *"In my defenselessness my safety lies."* And if ever someone comes along and irritates you or accuses you of something, making you feel compelled to stand up for yourself—it is far best not to do so. Just repeat mentally one of the lessons mentioned above and smile at the person in front of you, knowing that, in reality, he is your teacher, giving you the opportunity to choose once again—to choose between the ego or the Holy Spirit when you respond to him. The choice is yours.

CHAPTER 6

FEELING RESENTFUL OR UNFORGIVING

There will always be people who don't get on well with others; personality clashes are commonplace, especially in the work environment. The thing to remember is that they are just that—personality clashes. This really means *ego* clashes and, as long as we function merely as egos, there will always be conflict because the ego's thought system is based on fear and guilt. It would be unrealistic to expect things to be otherwise.

But it is possible to gain a new perspective on this. Given that all of us on earth are here because we believe we are egos, it makes sense to view each other with compassion and non-judgment. We are all struggling and striving to eke out an existence in a meaningless world doing meaningless things, and most of us are unaware of this. And given the fact that the ego projects its innate fear and guilt onto others to make it feel better about itself, then in a busy work environment one can imagine just how much projection and judgment must be taking place all the time. The only way to come to terms with this sorry state of affairs is to view each other with compassion and to remember that we are all one being, appearing to be separate individuals.

Lesson 73: "*I will there be light,*" serves as a useful reminder that darkness (in the form of judgment and grievances, for example) is not the will of God, And for those who are trying to live a life in conformity with the will of God it is helpful to remember that the light of God is there to help them, provided they are willing to let it into their minds. Lesson 73 mentions the ego's difficulty in getting on with others and points out: "*Idle wishes and grievances are partners or co-makers in picturing the world you see. The wishes of the ego gave rise to it, and the ego's need for grievances, which are necessary to maintain it, peoples it with figures that seem to attack you and call for 'righteous' judgment...Your will is lost to you in this strange bartering, in which guilt is traded back and forth, and grievances increase with each exchange. Can such a world have been created by the Will the*

Son of God shares with his Father?"

The ego wants us to believe that the world in which we live is Heaven because it does not want us to look for Heaven elsewhere. If we realize that this is just a dream and that Heaven is nowhere to be found on earth, there is every chance that we will awaken from the dream, and that would mean the demise of the ego. Yet Jesus tells us categorically that the world of the ego is *hell*, and if we want to end our suffering then we have to listen to the Voice for God—the Holy Spirit.

Whenever we are troubled the following can help give us peace of mind: *"I will there be light. Darkness is not my will."* And, having mentally repeated that a few times, it then makes sense to walk away from a situation of conflict and to try not to have anything more to do with it. Granted this is may not be easy, but with practice it becomes easier.

Lesson 75: *"The light has come,"* is a positive and uplifting lesson that follows on well from Lesson 73. In this lesson Jesus tells us that we are healed because, by being forgiving, we have let the light penetrate our minds and heal us. And in being healed ourselves, we can help others to heal. If we are feeling troubled because of the words or deeds of another, we should promptly repeat to ourselves: *"The light has come. I have forgiven you."* And if a situation is upsetting, the advice is to: *"Dwell not upon the past today. Keep a completely open mind, washed of all past ideas and clean of every concept you have made. You have forgiven the world today. You can look upon it now as if you never saw it before...."* Then we are asked to repeat several times: *"The light has come. I have forgiven the world."*

A Course in Miracles repeatedly asserts that the Holy Spirit will stand by us and help us if we take the first step by being forgiving to all and everyone. In most work environments there are ample opportunities to practice forgiveness, and there are many forgiveness lessons to be learnt. So, we could consider our workplace to be the perfect place to make spiritual progress and, although it is natural to prefer to work in a friendly, harmonious environment, we could embrace any conflict we find ourselves embroiled in because it is an opportunity to forgive. The same could be said for a difficult relationship we may be in. Eventually, when all our forgiveness lessons are over and done with, we will not find ourselves in difficult situations or in challenging relationships.

Initially, forgiveness takes a lot of hard work and practice. This phase could, in fact, last for many years. But the time must come when we won't have to actually stop and think about it—we automatically forgive and forget whenever we need to. Forgiving will have become our second nature, which is a worthy goal to work towards. In Chapter 17 of the Text we find this really nice definition of forgiveness: *"To forgive is merely to remember only the loving thoughts you gave in the past, and those that were given you. All the rest must be forgotten..."*[11] We need to remember only the loving thoughts and the kind deeds of others, and forget whatever else we may have experienced. If we can do this, it will mean that we only carry happy memories around with us, and that's a lovely thought.

Apart from forgiveness being a tool to awaken from the dream, it also, in the short run, gives us peace of mind. Once you have forgiven someone you feel as though a weight has been lifted off your shoulders and you can heave a sigh of relief. If it doesn't bring peace of mind with it, then the forgiveness lesson has not been properly applied and learnt. In *The Song of Prayer* we are told not to try to evaluate a situation or error that calls for forgiveness but to simply trust that forgiveness, without argument, is what is needed. *"All forms forgiveness takes that do not lead away from anger, condemnation and comparisons of every kind are death. For that is what their purposes have set. Be not deceived by them, but lay them by as worthless in their tragic offerings. You do not want to stay in slavery."*[12]

Nobody wants to stay in slavery. The light has come to make sure we don't. It's up to us if we let it into our minds or not.

---

[11] *ACIM*, T354.

[12] *The Song of Prayer—An Extension of the Principles of A Course in Miracles,*
   p. 13, Foundation for Inner Peace, California, 2007.

CHAPTER 7

FEELING LOST AND WANTING TO DISCOVER YOUR DIVINE PURPOSE

The problem with becoming an *A Course in Miracles* student is that as your perceptions of the world change (and they undoubtedly will), you may become rather disillusioned with life as you have been living it. Gradually, you realize that things that were meaningful in the past no longer seem to be as rewarding as they once were. It could be your job, travelling, shopping, going to the theatre or going out for a meal with friends. Although all these may still be pleasant experiences, you may find that you become rather ambivalent towards them—you can take them or leave them.

Another change one notices as one studies the Course is that there is a strong desire to do something that will help others awaken from the dream. This is probably true of many other spiritual paths as well. We find ourselves wondering whether it is our divine purpose to lead our fellowmen to the truth or whether God has a plan for us. So we think perhaps we should organize workshops or spiritual study groups or write a book, etc.

What should we do? *A Course in Miracles* does give clear guidance on this matter. Starting with Lesson 98: *"I will accept my part in God's plan for salvation,"* we see that God does have a plan for us and that we have a *"mighty purpose to fulfill..."* Similarly, Lesson 192 states *"I have a function God would have me fill."* And what is that function? It is forgiveness. *"Forgiveness represents your function here...Forgiveness gently looks upon all things unknown in Heaven, sees them disappear, and leaves the world a clean and unmarked slate on which the Word of God can now replace the senseless symbols written there before..."* Could it be that most or all of the things we are preoccupied with are merely *senseless symbols*?

One further lesson makes it very clear that by practicing forgiveness we are living in accordance with our divine purpose. Furthermore, it will lead to our enlightenment or salvation, as the

Course calls it. Lesson 99: *"Salvation is my only function here."* This lesson is perhaps one of the most important of all because it makes the connection between forgiveness and salvation crystal clear. *"Salvation and forgiveness are the same. They both imply that something has gone wrong; something to be saved from, forgiven for; something amiss that needs corrective change; something apart or different from the Will of God...Salvation now becomes the borderland between the truth and the illusion. It reflects the truth because it is the means by which you can escape illusions. Yet it is not yet the truth because it undoes what was never done."* Salvation or forgiveness undoes what was never done because the ego and the world of duality are illusions; we just think they exist. We need this important tool because we believe that the world of duality is real. *"...The mind that sees illusions thinks them real. They have existence in that they are thoughts. And yet they are not real, because the mind that thinks these thoughts is separate from God."*

Lesson 99 explains that we can be saved from our illusions if we practice forgiveness, and this includes forgiveness of ourselves as well as others. We need to forgive ourselves for having had the *"tiny, mad idea"* that resulted in the apparent separation from God and the creation of the ego. *"Forgive what you have made and you are saved."*

God has a plan to help us bring truth to our illusions—a plan which joins our separated minds with His Mind. But we need to turn to the Holy Spirit because, *"The Holy Spirit holds this plan of God exactly as it was received of Him within the Mind of God and in your own. It is apart from time in that its Source is timeless. Yet it operates in time, because of your belief that time is real. Unshaken does the Holy Spirit look on what you see; on sin and pain and death, on grief and separation and on loss. Yet does He know one thing must still be true; God is still Love, and this is not His Will. This is the Thought that brings illusions to the truth..."*[13] Forgiveness is God's plan for us. It will enable us to bring illusions to the truth which will awaken us from the dream, conquer the ego and liberate us.

If we go ahead and organize spiritual study groups, workshops, meetings, etc., or write a book which deals with some aspect of the

---

[13] *ACIM*, W177.

Course, it is perfectly all right. All these things are extremely helpful as they may help others awaken and hasten their journey Home. Yet, forgiveness has to be at the forefront of our minds every single day of our lives because it will definitely take us Home.

It is interesting to see what Ken Wapnick has to say on the matter. *"Whenever you feel you have important work to do in this world—e.g., a specific function Jesus has given you—you should smile knowingly and gently, realizing your ego has done it again. Your only function is to forgive...Our only important work is to change the mind that thinks there is a world..."*[14]

This means we can go about our daily lives as usual. We don't need to change our careers, our partners, our friends, our leisure time pursuits or the places where we go on holiday. All we need to do is to use these situations and relationships to practice forgiveness. Our daily lives become our spiritual practice. And if ever we feel unforgiving, we can quietly remind ourselves: *"I will accept my part in God's plan for salvation,"*[15] or *"Forgiveness ends the dream of conflict here,"* or *"Forgiveness is my function as the light of the world."*[16] Then smile.

A Course in Miracles can be studied and practiced in whatever circumstances we find ourselves, as mentioned in the preceding paragraph; there is no need for great changes to take place in our lives. Yet, as we progress with the Course, it is likely that *we* will change gradually and this, in turn, may lead to changes in our experiences and circumstances in life. The reason we will change is that when we make God our only goal, other goals will gradually become less and less important until they are given up altogether. This is explained in the Workbook: *"The full acceptance of salvation as your only function necessarily entails two phases; the recognition of salvation as your function. And the relinquishment of all the other goals you have invented for yourself."*[17] Remember that goals such as an education, career, family, travel, etc., are goals we have made up for ourselves

---

[14] Kenneth Wapnick, *The Healing Power of Kindness, Vol. Two*, p.108, *Foundation for A Course in* Miracles, Temecula, CA, 2005.

[15] *ACIM*, W174.

[16] *ACIM*, W104.

[17] *ACIM*, W108.

within the dream. Although they seem important to us when we are asleep, when we begin to awaken they no longer have the same appeal as before.

Although *ACIM* puts forgiveness first and foremost, it also asks us to be messengers of God. In Lesson 154 we read, *"...He needs our voice that He may speak through us. He needs our hands to hold His messages, and carry them to those whom He appoints. He needs our feet to bring us where He wills, that those who wait in misery may be at last delivered. And He needs our will united with His Own, that we may be the true receivers of the gifts He gives."* In sharing love, forgiveness and the truth with others, we receive these mighty gifts ourselves.

CHAPTER 8

WORRYING ABOUT ILL HEALTH AND EXPERIENCING PAIN

We only really start to worry about ill health when we begin to realize that our health, like everything else in the world of duality, is subject to change. For years and years we could enjoy good health and then, suddenly, out of the blue, along comes an ailment—maybe an allergy or a digestive complaint or something much more serious. It's then that we realize that our bodies are going to let us down eventually however much we look after ourselves, eat healthy food, take regular exercise and avoid pollutants.

Why, one might ask, did God create us mortals with bodies that will ultimately experience ill health and inevitably expire? The answer is He did not. But we may have difficulty believing this because so many religions tell us that God did create the universe and everything in it, including human beings. *A Course in Miracles* offers a very different and radical view on the matter—a view that makes much more sense.

According to *ACIM*, God did create us, but he created us as eternal, immortal spirit, one with Him and with each other. Then, at the time of the (perceived) separation from God or the fall, the mind (which is the creative aspect of the spirit) split into two portions, the wrong portion choosing to live apart from God. The ego was then created by the wrong mind, as an alternative to God; the ego then created, by projection, the human body, linear time and the universe in which to hide from God. And then, to top it all, we developed collective amnesia and completely forgot that we had ever been one with God. We had descended from non-duality into duality, from the real to the unreal and from immortality to mortality. Of course our bodies are going to perish in the end! Fortunately for us the creation of the body and the world of form, took place only at the level of the mind, and not in reality. We are still at home with God but are not aware of this because we have fallen asleep and are dreaming the dreams of the ego.

"...The body is a tiny fence around a little part of a glorious and complete idea. It draws a circle, infinitely small, around a very little segment of Heaven, splintered from the whole, proclaiming that within it is your kingdom, where God can enter not. Within this kingdom the ego rules, and cruelly..."[18] The world of the ego *is* a cruel world—a world where there is so much suffering and despair. And we will continue to suffer as long as we identify with our physical bodies. *"The body is the ego's idol; the belief in sin made flesh and then projected outward. This produces what seems to be a wall of flesh around the mind, keeping it prisoner in a tiny spot of space and time, beholden unto death, and given but an instant in which to sigh and grieve and die in honor of its master* (i.e., the ego). *And this unholy instant seems to be life; an instant of despair, a tiny island of dry sand, bereft of water and set uncertainly upon oblivion. Here does the Son of God stop briefly by, to offer his devotion to death's idols and then pass on. And here he is more dead than living..."*[19] If this beautifully written passage portrays a world that is bleak and sorrowful, we must remember that we could choose the *"holy instant"* to help us escape from our prison—a prison created by the ego in an unholy instant.

The holy instant is the instant we choose to turn to the Holy Spirit to ask Him to help us overcome the ego; we ask Him to help us undo the subconscious guilt in our minds and rise above the judgment and attack strategies of the ego, so that we can experience the miracle of forgiveness. We need to forgive ourselves and others, and each time we do so we are siding with the Holy Spirit and taking gradual steps towards awakening from the dream.

In the Manual for Teachers we are told that God's teachers are aware that sickness of the body is as unreal as good health of the body, because they know that the world of physical bodies is merely a dream world. *"...They* (God's teachers) *watch the dream figures come and go, shift and change, suffer and die. Yet they are not deceived by what they see. They recognize that to behold a dream figure as sick and*

---

[18] *ACIM,* T391.
[19] *ACIM,* T438.

separate is no more real than to regard it as healthy and beautiful... "[20]

There are a number of reasons why the physical body succumbs to ill health. Firstly, it could be the ego's way of forcing us to focus on the physical body, thus making it more difficult for us to awaken. As we read in the Text, *"Pain demonstrates the body must be real. It is a loud, obscuring voice whose shrieks would silence what the Holy Spirit says, and keep His words from your awareness. Pain compels attention, drawing it away from Him and focusing upon itself."*[21] Secondly, it could be a "poor me" strategy employed by the devious ego, which sees itself as a victim of the world and not responsible for its own suffering. *"Suffering is an emphasis upon all that the world has done to injure you....he sees himself attacked unjustly and by something not himself. He is the victim of this 'something else,' a thing outside himself, for which he has no reason to be held responsible..."*[22] Thirdly, ill health could be caused by subconscious guilt or anger projected onto one's own body instead of being projected outwards onto others. *"Sickness is anger taken out upon the body, so that it will suffer pain..."*[23] And in Lesson 140 we read: *"Sickness where guilt is absent cannot come, for it is but another form of guilt..."* We shouldn't really feel guilty because the separation from God didn't actually happen. But we do feel guilty because we don't know that; in fact, according to some teachers of *ACIM*, all the guilt we experience in our lives stems from the initial guilt that we experienced when we split away from Heaven.

Guilt is dealt with at length in the Course as it is seen as the source of all our troubles. In Chapter 5, Section V, it is explained that illness is caused by the ego because of the guilt it feels. These guilty feelings make the ego fearful of the wrath of God and so it chooses to punish itself by inflicting illness upon itself: *"I said before that illness is a form of magic. It might be better to say that it is a form of magical solution. The ego believes that by punishing itself it will mitigate the*

---

[20] *ACIM,* M32.

[21] *ACIM,* T579.

[22] *ACIM,* T581.

[23] *ACIM,* T603.

punishment of God... "[24]

Whatever the cause of physical ailments, the cure lies always in the mind. *ACIM* makes it very clear that healing can only ever take place in the mind, and never in the body. We are told that once we realize that we gain nothing from sickness, healing will take place. But the following passage explains why it is not easy for us to be healed. *"...First, it is obvious that decisions are of the mind, not of the body. If sickness is but a faulty problem-solving approach, it is a decision. And if it is a decision, it is the mind and not the body that makes it. The resistance to recognizing this is enormous, because the existence of the world as you perceive it depends on the body being the decision maker...The acceptance of sickness as a decision of the mind, for a purpose for which it would use the body, is the basis of healing. And this is so for healing in all forms. A patient decides that this is so and he recovers. If he decides against recovery, he will not be healed. Who is the physician? Only the mind of the patient himself..."* [25]

The Course makes it very clear that until we recognize that we are one with others we will not heal. However, if we can overlook the body, which makes us believe we are all separate from each other, and we are able to join with others at the level of the mind, then healing is definitely possible. In Chapter 28 it is explained that all those who identify with their physical bodies have made a secret vow with others to remain separate individuals. And the body represents the gap between the right and wrong portions of the mind. *"Whoever says, 'There is no gap between my mind and yours' has kept God's promise, not his tiny oath to be forever faithful unto death. And by his healing is his brother healed."* [26]

It isn't easy to disregard the body as it seems to be the focus of everything we do. But by continually reminding ourselves that we are eternal spirit and our bodies are just an image, we may gradually be able to change our perception of ourselves. It is likely that as we take steps to awaken from the dream and free ourselves from the ego, we will identify less with our physical bodies.

---

[24] *ACIM*, T84.

[25] *ACIM*, Manual for Teachers (M), p.17.

[26] *ACIM*, T603.

How can we use the Workbook to help us overcome the challenges imposed on us by sickness? Lesson 210 is very helpful: *"I am not a body, I am free. For I am still as God created me. I choose the joy of God instead of pain. Pain is my own idea. It is not a Thought of God, but one I thought apart from Him and from His Will..."* This lesson helps us remember that any pain and suffering we are going through has nothing to do with God but is of our own doing. It helps us take responsibility for our circumstances. Then we can ask for the guidance of the Holy Spirit and move on to Lesson 215: *"...The Holy Spirit is my only Guide. He walks with me in love. And I give thanks to Him for showing me the way to go."* So, in this way, we turn the problem over to a higher power, which should help minimize our anxiety and fear.

Of course it is all right when we are ill and in pain to resort to medication, pain relief, surgery, spiritual healing or any other form of external help, even though the Course refers to these as *"magic,"* because whilst we believe we are in a body, external agents such as these may help. However, if they help, it is because our *minds* have decided to allow the healing of the body to take place.

Lesson 140 is another very useful lesson to use in times of ill health. *"Only salvation can be said to cure."* It is interesting to note that this lesson deals with our "magical" means of healing our bodies, and it points out that unless we heal our minds through forgiveness, we will never really overcome sickness. Speaking of the remedies we use, the Course states: *"He is not healed. He merely had a dream that he was sick, and in the dream he found a magic formula to make him well. Yet he has not awakened from the dream, and so his mind remains exactly as it was before. He has not seen the light that would awaken him and end the dream. What difference does the content of a dream make in reality? One either sleeps or wakens. There is nothing in between."*[27] In other words, there really isn't much point trying to overcome a sick body *if we still remain stuck in the ego's dream world*. It makes much more sense to heal our minds completely and awaken from the dream by accepting the Atonement (recognition that the separation from God never took place.) That's why this lesson insists *"only salvation can be said to cure."*

---

[27] *ACIM*, W270.

The following passage (quoted briefly earlier on in this chapter) in Lesson 140 explains most lucidly the link between sickness and guilt: *"...Sickness where guilt is absent cannot come, for it is but another form of guilt. Atonement does not heal the sick, for that is not a cure. It takes away the guilt that makes the sickness possible. And that is cure indeed..."* Atonement will enable us to realize that we have never left Heaven and that we are all joined as one. This will eradicate our guilt, and the outcome will be good health.

However, for those of us who haven't reached the stage where we can suddenly awaken from the dream and return Home in an instant, and who have to gradually experience the miracle of forgiveness in small steps, it does make sense to use a little *"magic"* to help us overcome pain and ill health. Chronic pain is debilitating and needs to be dealt with. If we are in severe pain it will be practically impossible to remember that our bodies are unreal; so pain relief is essential in these circumstances. Forgiveness is equally important; we need to forgive ourselves for the guilt (which could be unconscious guilt) that is causing our sickness.

On the other hand, we also need to bear in mind that, in reality, we are free because we are not bodies; we are immortal spirit which can never be harmed regardless of what appears to be happening to the body in the dream. It may be helpful to tell oneself that although my body is sick, *I* am not. My body may be declining in health and strength but my Self (spirit) continues oblivious of all this.

"Only salvation can be said to cure."

CHAPTER 9

BEING AFRAID OF DEATH

Death is a particularly difficult topic to write about. It is our ultimate destiny and the unavoidable fate of all living creatures. We notice that everything in our world is destined to be born, grow, wither and die, and there's nothing we can do about it. It is generally a subject most people feel uncomfortable discussing, and yet there is something vitally important about death that we need to know and we need to tell ourselves every day: *despite appearances to the contrary, death is an impossibility.*

Jesus tells us in *A Course in Miracles* that, *"Death is the central dream from which all illusions stem. Is it not madness to think of life as being born, aging, losing vitality, and dying in the end? ....It is the one fixed, unchangeable belief of the world that all things in it are born only to die. This is regarded as 'the way of nature,' not to be raised to question, but to be accepted as the 'natural' law of life....all this is taken as the Will of God. And no one asks if a benign Creator could will this."*[28]

If we sit down and ponder on this we will come to the inevitable conclusion that a loving God would not create mortal human beings simply to have them end their lives in weakness and sickness before dying. All the religions that teach this must believe that God is cruel and vindictive and definitely not a *"benign Creator."* A God of love would give us eternal life, and for those who believe in non-duality this is exactly what they are certain He has done. He has created us as immortal spirit, one with Him and with all of creation, and it is *not* His will for us to be born as mortals and then die. This is repeated numerous times in *A Course in Miracles.*

In the following passage Jesus points out that death is only real to us because we identify with our bodies; we think we are our bodies. *"The 'reality' of death is firmly rooted in the belief that God's Son is a*

---

[28] *ACIM,* M66.

body. And if God created bodies, death would indeed be real. But God would not be loving.... " Then Jesus refers to a passage in the Bible, and he explains its true meaning: *" 'And the last to be overcome will be death.' Of course! Without the idea of death there is no world. All dreams will end with this one. This is salvation's final goal; the end of all illusions. And in death are all illusions born. What can be born of death and still have life? But what can be born of God and still can die?"*[29]

In Chapter 19 of the Text it is explained that there is no body and so it follows that there can be no such thing as death. *"The body no more dies than it can feel. It does nothing. Of itself it is neither corruptible nor incorruptible. It **is** nothing. It is the result of a tiny, mad idea of corruption that can be corrected. For God has answered this insane idea with His Own..."*[30] God's answer was the creation of the Holy Spirit Who has remained with us ever since.

Another reason why death is not possible is that we are all holy Sons of God; this is a key theme in *A Course in Miracles*. The term Son of God is not reserved solely for Jesus but is something we all share with him. If we are holy Sons of God then we, like Jesus, must have been given the gift of eternal life. In Lesson 198 we are told that it is insanity to think that God condemns us (for the separation) and also to believe that we can die: *"...How mad to think that you could be condemned, and that the holy Son of God can die!"*[31]

Despite being aware of the above, it is probably true to say that the thought of the death of the body *is* frightening because, in the world of form, we have identified with it for so long. To help us overcome this fear, faith in the teachings of Jesus (and other enlightened spiritual teachers) is essential. One could talk for hours about the unreality of death but one has no actual proof of this. So faith is needed, but there are a few lessons in the Workbook that can also help.

One such lesson is Lesson 163: *"There is no death. The Son of God is free."* This lesson points out that death appears to be the one certain thing in our lives but it is an impossibility because, *"... For*

---

[29] *ACIM*, M67.

[30] *ACIM*, T418.

[31] *ACIM*, W380.

death is total. Either all things die, or else they live and cannot die. No compromise is possible....The idea of the death of God is so preposterous that even the insane have difficulty believing it. For it implies that God was once alive and somehow perished; killed, apparently, by those who did not want Him to survive. Their stronger will could triumph over His, and so eternal life gave way to death. And with the Father died the Son as well. "[32] This refers to the beliefs of the ego, which created the world of form and the physical body to take the place of God and Heaven, hoping God could be vanquished in this way. *But this did not happen.*

The following upbeat passage on page 616 of the Text is worth reading whenever the fear of death enters one's mind: *"Swear not to die, you holy Son of God! You cannot make a bargain that you cannot keep. The Son of Life cannot be killed. He is immortal as his Father. What he is cannot be changed. He is the only thing in all the universe that must be one. What* **seems** *eternal all will have an end. The stars will disappear, and night and day will be no more. All things that come and go, the tides, the seasons and the lives of men; all things that change with time and bloom and fade will not return. Where time has set an end is not where the eternal is. God's Son can never change by what men made of him. He will be as he was and as he is, for time appointed not his destiny, nor set the hour of his birth and death. Forgiveness will not change him. Yet time waits upon forgiveness that the things of time may disappear because they have no use."* This passage stresses that all the things in the world of duality, miscreated by the ego, will come to an end at some point, but *we will not* because we are immortal spirit—we are not our bodies. Forgiveness is the tool to use to bring to an end all the illusions of the ego; then we will revert to (or remember) our true state—eternal spirit.

Lesson 167, *"There is one life, and that I share with God,"* gives the following definition of death: *"Death is the thought that you are separate from your Creator. It is the belief conditions change, emotions alternate because of causes you cannot control....It is the fixed belief ideas can leave their source, and take on qualities the source does not contain, becoming different from their own origin,*

---

[32]*ACIM,* W310.

apart from it in kind as well as distance, time and form. "[33] But ideas *cannot* leave their source, as we read in the next paragraph: *"Death cannot come from life. Ideas remain united to their source."* This last sentence is repeated many times throughout the Course and it is a key concept that mustn't be forgotten. It is because *"ideas leave not their source"* that we cannot die. We are simply an idea in the mind of God and, as such, we share His characteristics. Since God is eternal and immortal, so are we. We cannot assume a physical form which eventually dies. Lesson 167 tells us, *"What seems to die is but the sign of mind asleep."* When we awaken from our dream we will no longer experience death.

Lesson 95 is also useful in helping us overcome the fear of death. *"I am one Self, united with my Creator."* This lesson explains that we are one with all creation and this unity makes change impossible. What God created must be eternal like Himself. As death is the most extreme form of change that we experience on earth, death must also be impossible. We can use the following affirmation in Lesson 95 to reassure ourselves: *"I am one Self, united with my Creator, at one with every aspect of creation, and limitless in power and in peace."* Instead of being anxious about dying, we could focus on awakening in *this* lifetime so that we don't have to come back and experience death again. If we can achieve this, then the death of our physical body in this lifetime will lead us beyond birth and death and into eternity.

---

[33] *ACIM*, W318.

CHAPTER 10

FEELING MISTRUSTFUL ABOUT SOMEONE

Lesson 181 tells us quite clearly that we should trust each other: *"I trust my brothers, who are one with me."* On the face of it, this seems a rather strange thing to do given the way we treat each other and all the acts of violence we inflict upon each other. Is this lesson telling us not to bother to bolt our front doors at night, or lock the car or avoid walking alone down deserted alleyways late at night? Not really. This lesson is actually concerned with changing our perceptions of each other so that we recognize that we are not separate individuals inhabiting millions of physical bodies. We are asked to ignore the perceived errors of others because, in reality, they only occur in the dream of life on earth.

So, despite the often horrible things one human being does to another, we are told that none of us are guilty because these things are not actually happening; we remain sinless as we were when God created us. *"If God knows His children as wholly sinless, it is blasphemous to perceive them as guilty. If God knows His children as wholly without pain, it is blasphemous to perceive suffering anywhere....If God created His Son perfect, that is how you must learn to see him to learn of his reality. And as part of the Sonship, that is how you must see yourself to learn of yours."*[34]

A Course in Miracles asks us to see the light of God in all others, regardless of what their egos may be doing; we need to overlook all their deeds—however horrific they may be—and focus on the fact that we are *all* holy Sons of God. If we see others as sinless, we will experience peace; if we choose to judge and condemn them for their deeds in the dream, we will experience pain, as Lesson 351 explains clearly: *"My sinless brother is my guide to peace. My sinful brother is my guide to pain. And which I choose to see I will behold."* This is another useful lesson to use when we need reminding to trust one

---

[34] *ACIM,* T192.

another.

It is helpful to remember that any physical or verbal abuse is simply a cry for help from someone who has lost his way Home. With reference to the Holy Spirit we read in Chapter 12: *"...Having taught you to accept only loving thoughts in others and to regard everything else as an appeal for help, He has taught you that fear itself is an appeal for help...Fear is a symptom of your own deep sense of loss. If when you perceive it in others you learn to supply the loss, the basic cause of fear is removed. Thereby you teach yourself that fear does not exist in you. The means for removing it is in yourself, and you have demonstrated this by giving it. Fear and love are the only emotions of which you are capable..."*[35] This implies that whenever we feel frightened we need to be brave and offer love instead of attack. (But this doesn't mean we don't continue to try to protect our bodies and homes.) It is a matter of trying to focus on the holiness of others rather than on the deeds their bodies may perform out of fear. *"...See no one as a body. Greet him as the Son of God he is, acknowledging that he is one with you in holiness."*[36]

---

[35] *ACIM*, T217.
[36] *ACIM*, W299.

CHAPTER 11

UNABLE TO MEDITATE AND CALM THE MIND

Although *A Course in Miracles* does not focus specifically on the need to meditate, there are several sections in the Text and Workbook which deal with the need to turn away from the outer world and concentrate on the world within. And, whilst daily meditation sessions are not strictly required, it is evident that Jesus does ask us to have regular moments of calm to help us rise above the unending stream of ego-based thoughts that flow through the mind.

Meditation is not an easy thing to do however long one practices; the cares and concerns of our busy lifestyle frequently intrude upon our minds when we sit down in search of calm, inner peace and guidance. The more we rush around during the day trying to get numerous things done, the more active we may find our minds are when we actually stop to meditate.

Fortunately, there are a number of lessons in the Workbook which can be used to help calm the mind and control the thoughts that seem to whirl through the mind in a frenzy. *"Let me be still and listen to the truth,"* we read in Lesson 106. This lesson warns us that ego will try to distract us, but if we can turn away from it we will hear the Voice for God. *"If you will lay aside the ego's voice, however loudly it may seem to call; if you will not accept its petty gifts that give you nothing that you really want; if you will listen with an open mind, that has not told you what salvation is; then you will hear the mighty Voice of truth, quiet in power, strong in stillness, and completely certain in Its messages."*[37]

If one meditates after a busy day at work one may find that all the issues that cropped up during the day return to occupy the mind. Then, after going beyond these thoughts, it may be possible to turn within and experience some moments of tranquility. However, if a meal has to be cooked in the evening, one may find that one's mind wanders off

---

[37] *ACIM,* W190.

to the kitchen and starts to plan the meal. This, of course, is just another ego tactic, but it is quite difficult to conquer if one is hungry. Yet, Lesson 106 urges us to continue with our meditation: *"Be not afraid to circumvent the voices of the world. Walk lightly past their meaningless persuasion. Hear them not. Be still today and listen to the truth..."*

Lesson 221 is another suitable lesson to use when one tries to turn within and shut out the raucous ego. *"Peace to my mind. Let all my thoughts be still."* This lesson emphasizes the need to calm the mind so that we can receive guidance from the Voice for God.

Another lesson which clearly shows the need to calm the mind in order to hear the truth is Lesson 291. *"This is a day of stillness and of peace."* That statement could be used throughout the day, particularly on a hectic day when one is rushing around not experiencing peace. It would just take a second or two to stop everything and repeat that lesson quietly to oneself. Lesson 291 continues, *"This day my mind is quiet, to receive the Thoughts You offer me. And I accept what comes from You, instead of myself..."* If one is feeling agitated for whatever reason, then forgiveness is the antidote. As Lesson 291 explains, if we offer forgiveness to people or situations that trouble us, we will experience peace. If we can do this, we will be looking upon the world with *"Christ's vision."* We must also forgive ourselves for our limitations and for whatever it is we may have done to disturb our peace of mind.

It is interesting to note that one of the main motivations for becoming a student of *A Course in Miracles* is to experience peace; the more forgiving we become, the more peaceful we become, and then we are able to acquire knowledge. *"Knowledge is not the motivation for learning this course. Peace is. This is the prerequisite for knowledge only because those who are in conflict are not peaceful, and peace is the condition of knowledge because it is the condition of the Kingdom..."*[38]

Lesson 49, *"God's Voice speaks to me all through the day,"* is a lovely lesson, which asks us try to shut off the part of the mind that listens to the ego so that we can hear God's Voice. With reference to

---

[38] *ACIM*, T138.

our split minds we read, *"The part that is listening to the Voice for God is calm, always at rest and wholly certain. It is really the only part there is. The other part is a wild illusion, frantic and distraught, but without any reality of any kind. Try today not to listen to it. Try to identify with the part of your mind where stillness and peace reign forever. Try to hear God's Voice call to you lovingly, reminding you that your Creator has not forgotten his Son."*[39] This passage highlights the importance of finding the time for moments of meditation or at least for moments of tranquility in which we are able to go within and ignore the doings of the ego.

The following passage also emphasizes how important it is to have a calm mind if we want to experience the miracle of forgiveness. *"The miracle comes quietly into the mind that stops an instant and is still. It reaches gently from that quiet time, and from the mind it healed in quiet then, to other minds to share its quietness. And they will join in doing nothing to prevent its radiant extension back into the Mind which caused all minds to be..."*[40] This passage shows how a healed mind can heal other minds, since we are all joined. It goes on to explain that the memory of God will return to us (and thereby heal our minds) provided we take the time to be still.

It can be difficult to meditate in this day and age when we have so much going on in our lives as well as a huge information overload due to all our technological advances. For those who have difficulty meditating, there are many techniques which may help. One could focus on a mantra or focus on one's breath, and each time one becomes aware that the mind has wandered, simply return to focusing on the mantra or the breath. Listening to a meditation tape can be very helpful; there are recordings of binaural beats which, when used with stereo headphones, enable the brain to enter the relaxing alpha, delta and theta states. Sometimes walking peacefully alone in a forest or along the seashore is a good way to meditate or at least to calm the incessant thoughts that swirl through the mind. However, if one is in a very agitated state due being overworked or having a problem on the mind, then it is best to abandon one's meditation session and try to

---

[39] *ACIM*, W78.
[40] *ACIM*, T591.

resolve the problem before attempting to meditate again later on in the day when one is feeling calmer.

The Course teaches us that there is a bridge between our illusory world and Heaven, and in order to reach the bridge and cross over it, we need to find peace—the peace of God. With reference to all the distractions of the ego we read in Lesson 200, *"Peace is the bridge that everyone will cross, to leave this world behind...Peace is the answer to conflicting goals, to senseless journeys, frantic, vain pursuits, and meaningless endeavors. Now the way is easy, sloping gently toward the bridge where freedom lies within the peace of God."*[41]

We can only benefit by turning away, for a few moments every day, from our *"frantic, vain pursuits and meaningless endeavors,"* so as to achieve the goal of peace, and ultimately the goal of crossing over that bridge to Heaven. What could be more important than that?

---

[41] *ACIM*, W385.

CHAPTER 12

WORRYING ABOUT THE FUTURE

Planning is part of our basic nature as human beings; we plan what to do at the weekend; where to go on holiday; how much we want to save for the future; how many children we want to have; where and how we want to live, etc., etc. There is nothing wrong with making plans for future events but when the planning turns into worrying, then we have a problem that needs to be solved. The only really effective solution is to hand the problem over to the Holy Spirit as Lesson 194 asks us to do: *"I place the future in the Hands of God."* If we are really able to do this we will feel much more relaxed. Jesus tells us in Lesson 194, *"Accept today's idea, and you have passed all anxiety, all pits of hell, all blackness of depression, thoughts of sin, and devastation brought about by guilt."*

As we have seen, guilt is a major problem for all of us, and it stems from the initial act of separation from God eons ago. Guilt, in turn, leads to fear of punishment from God—punishment we believe we deserve and will receive. So we can see that the separation that took place in the past, leads to guilt in the present which translates into fear of the future because we are afraid of the wrath of God. That is why we read in Lesson 194: *"...You are but asked to let the future go, and place it in God's Hands. And you will see by your experience that you have laid the past and present in His Hands as well, because the past will punish you no more, and future dread will now be meaningless."* In other words, by handing our worries over to God we are, in some way, overcoming our original guilt due to the separation and, therefore, we no longer need to worry about being punished by God in the future. To *"let the future go,"* implies that are our apparent worries about health, wealth and happiness are not as important as we believe them to be. We must remember that they are all part of the dream in this illusory world. What is important though is overcoming our guilt and fear by turning all our worries over to God; we can do this by calling upon the Holy Spirit or Jesus.

Another important thing to remember is that we will never find long-term security and happiness in this world for the simple reason that *everything* is impermanent. One's physical body could be destroyed in an instant by an earthquake or by a disease; one's money could vanish overnight in a stock market crash. And even if everything goes smoothly throughout one's life, death is unavoidable. So it makes sense to try not to worry about our bodies, health and material possessions but to focus instead on awakening from the dream and returning Home.

Lesson 76 reminds us: *"I am under no laws but God's."* Repeating this lesson could help alleviate any worries we have about the future. Jesus explains very clearly in this lesson that all the things we worry about are, actually, unreal. *"You really think that you would starve unless you have stacks of green paper strips and piles of metal discs. You really think a small round pellet or some fluid pushed into your veins through a sharpened needle will ward off disease and death...It is insanity that thinks these things...You think you must obey the "laws" of medicine, or economics and of health. Protect the body, and you will be saved. These are not laws, but madness. The body is endangered by the mind that hurts itself...The body's suffering is a mask the mind holds up to hide what really suffers..."* What really suffers is the mind that split from the one mind and created the ego and the body. So it is our minds that need to be healed; when they are whole we will have awakened from our collective dream. In the meantime, repeating the phrase, *"I am under no laws but God's,"* will loosen the ego's control over our split or wrong mind. As Jesus explains, *"It is our statement of freedom from all danger and all tyranny."*

Another very helpful lesson, similar to Lesson 76, is Lesson 47: *"God is the strength in which I trust."* As egos we *are* vulnerable but as holy Sons of God we are not. So we read in Lesson 47, *"If you are trusting in your own strength, you have every reason to be apprehensive, anxious and fearful. What can you predict or control? What is there in you that can be counted on?"* It is explained that we need to understand that we are frail and weak if we rely upon our little selves for anything. But we also need to appreciate the fact that we have access to God's strength because God is in our minds and we are one with Him. *"God is your safety in every circumstance. His Voice speaks for Him in all situations and in every aspect of all situations, telling you exactly what to do to call upon His strength and His protection..."*

Jesus is not asking us to completely disregard the body; it *does* make sense within the dream, to earn one's living, save for the future, look after the body and provide shelter for it, etc. But it is important to remember that, firstly, this is just a dream or a mental projection and, secondly, the body needs to be preserved within the dream so that it can fulfill its only really important function, which is to be a means of communication and a tool for forgiveness. *"The Holy Spirit teaches you to use your body only to reach your brothers, so He can teach His message through you. This will heal them and therefore heal you..."*[42]

The body doesn't need to be used to accumulate great wealth; to create offspring; to become famous; or to excel in the workplace. It *may* do all these things and that's all right, but there is a more important use of the body than all these things—using it as a means of communication to bring about healing. So whilst it's natural to be concerned about security in the long-term and to make provision for a pension, financial security for old age, etc., *ACIM* is teaching us that no matter what plans we make, we cannot rely upon the body or the ego, and that we are only under God's laws.

It must give us peace of mind to trust in God so completely that we are not concerned about the welfare of the physical body. One would imagine that those whom the Course refers to as advanced teachers of God have probably reached that state. But for the rest of us, who are a little further behind on our spiritual journey, we can use the uplifting lessons of *A Course in Miracles* to help us recognize our true inner power and strength, which comes from our connection to God.

Lesson 292, *"A happy outcome to all things is sure"* is a happy way to end this chapter. It does not refer to all the things we believe will give us happiness in our world. It refers instead to the eternal joy to be found only in Heaven. *"God's promises make no exceptions. And He guarantees that only joy can be the final outcome found for everything. Yet it is up to us when this is reached; how long we let an*

---

[42] *ACIM*, T157.

alien will appear to be opposing His..." The alien will is, of course, the ego's will. And it is up to us to choose once again so that we can awaken from ego's dream and find eternal joy which we are entitled to as holy Sons of God.

CHAPTER 13

FEELING TRAPPED IN THE WORLD OF THE EGO

A Course in Miracles and many other great spiritual books tell us that the ego is unreal, yet it seems real to those who are living in the world of form. *ACIM* also tells us that the world of time and space are equally unreal, yet, they too, seem real. In fact, one might wonder how one can actually become consciously aware of the fact that the ego is unreal when every day of our lives, for lifetime after lifetime, we are guided by the ego. It could appear to us that we are trapped in the world of the ego with no way of awakening. Fortunately, this is not so.

If ever we do feel trapped, we need to realize that the first thing we must change is our perception because the only place we are trapped in is in our minds. But we can heal our split minds by changing our mind about the meaning of the world. When we realize that this world has no meaning, we begin to awaken. Lesson 23, *"I can escape from the world I see by giving up attack thoughts"* is helpful in that it reminds us that the world was initially miscreated by the attack thoughts of a split mind, which sought to escape from God and Heaven. In this lesson it is explained, *"The idea for today introduces the thought that you are not trapped in the world you see, because its cause can be changed..."* The cause is the apparent creation of the ego and the world by the wrong portion of the mind; if we can heal our split minds, we will be set free.

Something else we have to work hard at is overcoming guilt, as mentioned in the previous chapter. Guilt is a major ego device to keep us trapped here. *"...Love and guilt cannot coexist, and to accept one is to deny the other. Guilt hides Christ from your sight, for it is the denial of the blamelessness of God's Son....For the blamelessness of Christ is the proof that the ego never was, and can never be. Without guilt the ego has no life, and God's Son **is** without guilt."*[43] We need to keep

---

[43]*ACIM*, T237.

telling ourselves that we are *not* guilty, despite what we see in this illusory world. This is explained in the following paragraph, *"As you look upon yourself and judge what you do honestly, you may be tempted to wonder how you can be guiltless. Yet consider this: You are not guiltless in time, but in eternity. You have 'sinned' in the past, but there is no past..."* We sinned at the time of the separation when we created the ego; yet, as this did not really happen, we did not really sin. Thus, we are not guilty, and it is really helpful to dismiss any guilty thoughts from our minds as soon as they surface. We also need to make sure we don't let others lay a guilt trip on us.

People tend to take the things going on their lives very seriously. But if this world is just a mental projection it might be best not to. The ego would like us to believe that everything going on in the world is vitally important, but we need to listen to the ego much less, and turn instead to the Holy Spirit. Lesson 49, *"God's Voice speaks to me all through the day"* is a very useful lesson to use when trying to avoid ego thoughts. This lesson offers good advice: *"Listen in deep silence. Be very still and open your mind. Go past all the raucous shrieks and sick imaginings that cover your real thoughts and obscure your eternal link with God. Sink deep into the peace that waits for you beyond the frantic, riotous thoughts and sights and sounds of this insane world. You do not live here. We are trying to reach your real home. We are trying to reach the place where you are truly welcome. We are trying to reach God."* And this is what we must remember; we are trying to reach God.

It will help if we don't focus on the problems of the world. Watch the TV news only occasionally, and switch it off when the violence becomes too unbearable. Skim through the newspapers only once in a while, and remember it is all an illusion. If we focus on the suffering of others and on those who cause the suffering of others, we are making this dream world real, and we will never awaken. *A Course in Miracles* tells us frequently that instead of trying to change the world, we need to focus on changing our minds about the world. We need to change our thoughts because the world is simply a manifestation of our thoughts.

Further on in the Workbook we are advised to take time out from our world. What a welcome break that is. All those who meditate regularly must realize how wonderful it is to turn away from the world and go within, even if it is just for a few minutes every day. *"Thus what you need are intervals each day in which the learning of the world becomes a transitory phase; a prison house from which you go into the sunlight and forget the darkness."*[44] In these little moments of calm we can meditate or focus upon a particular Workbook lesson or simply tune into nature. What is important is that we take our minds off ourselves (the ego) and go within to a place that is beyond the body, beyond the ego and beyond time and space. A lesson we can use to help us in this regard is Lesson 182, *"I will be still an instant and go home."* This lesson explains that the world we live in is not our home, and the memory of our true home is always with us although we may not be aware of this. Being still will make it more likely that we receive guidance from Jesus or the Holy Spirit. *"When you are still an instant, when the world recedes from you, when valueless ideas cease to have value in your restless mind, then will you hear His Voice."*

Another lesson which will help us remember that we are not trapped in the world of the ego is Lesson 226, *"My home awaits me. I will hasten there."* This lesson explains that we can return to our true, pre-separation home by changing our mind about the purpose of the world. If we believe this world has value, when we will remain trapped in it. But if we can rise above it by knowing that it is unreal and that it has nothing of value to offer, then we can set ourselves free.

There must be many occasions when Course students ask themselves what it is that is holding them back. Why do they feel trapped in this imaginary world? Why can't they suddenly awaken and find themselves living in the real world? The answer can be found in the Manual: *"The resurrection is...the relinquishment of all other purposes, all other interests, all other wishes and all other concerns. It is the single desire of the Son for the Father."*[45] So the key is single-mindedness and detachment—making God our *only* goal, and gradually losing interest in our former way of life.

Even though we are not really trapped in this world, we are told that we need help to awaken from our dream world; we can't do it on

---

44 *ACIM,* W346.
45 *ACIM,* M68.

our own because our ego-based perceptions and beliefs have become so entrenched over the years and over lifetimes. *"The Holy Spirit, therefore, must begin His teaching by showing you what you can never learn. His message is not indirect, but He must introduce the simple truth into a thought system which has become so twisted and so complex you cannot see that it means nothing"*[46] We take our dream world seriously, and we really can't see that it lacks purpose and meaning. That's why we need a teacher who is outside our thought system such as the Holy Spirit or Jesus (the manifestation of the Holy Spirit.) It is, therefore, important to remember to call upon the Holy Spirit every day, especially when faced with problems or challenging situations. A useful affirmation in this regard is Lesson 327, *"I need but call and You will answer me."*[47]

The Holy Spirit is the mediator between the two worlds—our illusory world and Heaven. He is the link between the two, but we won't be able to make good use of His help unless we can detach, to some extent, from our world. Chapter 13 of the Text warns us that if we value things in this world, we will not escape from it. *"The world you see must be denied, for sight of it is costing you a different kind of vision. You cannot see both worlds, for each of them involves a different kind of seeing, and depends on what you cherish. The sight of one is possible because you have denied the other. Both are not true, yet either one will seem as real to you as the amount to which you hold it dear..."*[48] It is not easy to deny the world in which we live as our senses seem to prove to us that it exists. The only thing we can do is to frequently remind ourselves that our goal is to awaken from the dream. We can go about our daily activities as normal but, at the same time, try not to get too attached to anything in our lives.

Finally, forgiveness must be mentioned as it is this which will ultimately bring about our salvation or liberation. The following is one of the best definitions of forgiveness in *A Course in Miracles*: *"Forgiveness recognizes what you thought your brother did to you has not occurred. It does not pardon sins and make them real. It sees there*

---

[46] *ACIM*, T271.

[47] *ACIM*, W465.

[48] *ACIM*, T254.

was no sin. And in that view are all your sins forgiven."[49] This sums up the essence of the teachings of *ACIM* very clearly. We forgive others because we know that everything in this world is unreal and everyone is guiltless and holy. And we forgive ourselves for the same reason. Eventually, when we have completed all our forgiveness lessons we will find that we are no longer trapped in the world of the ego because we will have left the ego behind and returned in our awareness to our true state of oneness with God and all of creation.

---

[49] *ACIM,* W401.

CHAPTER 14

FEELING UNHAPPY, ANXIOUS OR AFRAID DUE TO DIFFICULT CIRCUMSTANCES

The Course teaches us that our thoughts determine the world we see. It is useful to remember that when we are in the midst of challenges and difficulties, because we may be tempted to blame others for our predicament. Instead, it is important to ask oneself why one has decided to manifest this particular situation in one's life. Is there something to be learnt from it? Do we need to learn how to be more patient or trusting or forgiving or loving or selfless?

Lesson 193 points out that, *"All things are lessons God would have me learn."* It is interesting to note that this lesson states that a lack of forgiveness is the cause of *all* our difficulties, even though that may not be apparent. *"Certain it is that all distress does not appear to be but unforgiveness. Yet that is the content underneath the form..."* This means that whatever we are unhappy or anxious about can be overcome by forgiveness. That's why we are told in Lesson 193, *"Forgive, and you will see this differently."* It is explained that, *"These are the words the Holy Spirit speaks in all your tribulations, all your pain, all suffering regardless of its form..."* So, whenever we feel unhappy or anxious or afraid for whatever reason, we can calm our minds by repeating to ourselves, *"I will forgive, and this will disappear."*

It is quite easy to become unhappy or disturbed when reading the newspapers or watching the news on television. What we are really watching is the ego projecting its guilt and fear onto others, which inevitably results in conflict. It doesn't matter which country the news is focusing on; it doesn't matter who the people are; and it doesn't matter which war is being waged. All that we need to be aware of is that we are witnessing the ego at work, and anything in the world of the ego is essentially meaningless. Lesson 12 is relevant in this situation: *"I am upset because I see a meaningless world."* And Lesson 11 makes us realize that it is our own thoughts that determine what we see: *"My meaningless thoughts are showing me a meaningless world."* When the world collectively becomes more loving, more forgiving and more peaceful, the images on our television screens will correspondingly become more loving, forgiving and peaceful.

We often find ourselves in situations in which we are at the mercy of others. To give one example, when moving house we have to wait to find someone who wants to buy our property, whilst we look for another suitable house for ourselves. We have to wait for the solicitors to carry out the necessary paperwork, and we have to wait for the bank or building society to do the same, and then release the funds, if we require a mortgage. This can be a very slow process, and all we can do is sit back and watch things unfold. During the process, the vendor may decide not to sell you the home you would like or the buyer may change his mind and withdraw his offer. If one is in a hurry to get this long process completed it can be quite a stressful time in one's life. In such a situation we may find that Lesson 248 is particularly useful: *"Whatever suffers is not part of me."* No matter how anxious or stressed out one may feel, it is important to recall that, *"...What grieves is not myself. What is in pain is but illusion in my mind..."* All one can do is to surrender the situation to a higher power and let things take their course whilst remembering that however stressed or unhappy we may feel at the present moment, we are really only living in a make-believe world. Yet, it may still not be easy and we will need to call upon the Holy Spirit for help. This important lesson, which was mentioned in the previous chapter, can be used once again: *"I need but call and You will answer me."*[50]

We are really calling upon Jesus or the Holy Spirit to help us realize that we are not this little, individual person who is experiencing stress or anxiety. We are asking to have the memory of our true Self be restored in our minds. In other words, we are asking to have our split minds healed.

Although we may be unhappy or anxious or afraid about something going on in our lives, our true Self, the *Son of God*, is always at peace. *"Like to the sun and ocean your Self continues,*

---

[50] *ACIM,* W465.

unmindful that this tiny part regards itself as you. It is not missing; it could not exist if it were separate, nor would the whole be whole without it...It leads no separate life, because its life is the oneness in which its being was created."[51] We are being reminded that our little individual self is really non-existent, and that we are still at one with God and all of creation. And we are being asked to disregard our lower self/personality and make use of the holy instant to invite love into our lives. *"The holy instant is your invitation to love to enter into your bleak and joyless kingdom, and to transform it into a garden of peace and welcome..."*[52]

Lesson 361 is a wonderful lesson to repeat when one is not feeling peaceful and happy:

"This holy instant would I give to You.
Be You in charge. For I would follow You,
Certain that Your direction gives me peace."

By repeating these words we are handing our problems over to the Holy Spirit and asking for His guidance.

---

[51] *ACIM*, T391.
[52] *ACIM*, T392.

CHAPTER 15

WHEN THINGS NO LONGER APPEAL TO YOU

If we think back to our youth there were many things that caused us excitement and happiness. Young children can spend hours blissfully playing with their toys, oblivious of anything else going on around them. For teenagers, clothes and boyfriends/girlfriends seem to be the most important things in the world. A little later on, having a successful career and a nice car come very high on our list of priorities. Not long after that, marriage and a family may become our major concern as well as saving up for a home of our own. That's probably how it is for the majority of people on this planet. And then, as we become a little older and wiser, we may begin to search for meaning and, if we are lucky, we will discover that life isn't about the things just mentioned; life is about awakening.

One of the first signs of awakening is a gradual loss of interest in things that previously seemed very important; our priorities begin to change as do our perception of the world and our opinions and beliefs. We may, at this stage, withdraw from the world a little, as going out socializing no longer seems to be as meaningful as it once was. If we reach this stage Lessons 128 and 129 may be very appropriate: *"The world I see holds nothing that I want"* and *"Beyond this world there is a world I want."* Whilst there will still be some things in this world of illusions that we enjoy and think we want, we are warned in Lesson 128, *"Each thing you value here is but a chain that binds you to the world, and it will serve no other end but this...Let nothing that relates to body thoughts delay your progress to salvation...Nothing here is worth one instant of delay and pain; one moment of uncertainty and doubt."*

We shouldn't become despondent about our loss of passion for certain things in life. Quite the contrary, it is a positive sign if it causes us to look beyond this world. As we read in Lesson 129, *"The world you see is merciless indeed, unstable, cruel, unconcerned with you, quick to avenge and pitiless with hate. It gives but to rescind, and takes away all things that you have cherished for a while."* How true that last sentence is. All the things we cherish will be taken from us sooner or later, even though we would like them to last forever.

Turning away from the so-called pleasures of this world does not really involve sacrifice if we remember that what we believe we are losing is no real loss at all. *"Is it a loss to find a world instead where losing is impossible; where love endures forever, hate cannot exist and vengeance has no meaning?"*[53] The only place where love endures forever is Heaven.

The Course frequently refers to us as being asleep; it is a sign that we are beginning to awaken if we begin to lose interest in some of the distractions set up by the ego to keep us focused on the world of form. In the Manual for Teachers we read, *"It takes great learning both to realize and to accept the fact the world has nothing to give. What can the sacrifice of nothing mean? It cannot mean that you have less because of it...Think a while about what the world calls sacrifice. Power, fame, money, physical pleasure...Could they mean anything except to a body?"*[54] But when we recall that we are not bodies, then it makes sense to gradually withdraw one's interest from the body and, therefore, from power, fame, money and physical pleasure. It doesn't seem like a sacrifice because it is not something we force upon ourselves; it seems to happen gradually on its own.

Growing weary of this world and trying to find a deeper meaning to life is normal if we want to grow as a spiritual being; if we don't grow we will become stagnant like a lifeless pond, and we will continue to do the same things day after day, month after month and year after year until the apparent end of our lives. Lesson 224, *"God is my Father, and He loves His Son"* is an uplifting lesson for those who feel disenchanted with the world of the ego. It reminds us of our only true goal—God—and it is reassuring because it also assures us that God loves us. In this lesson there is a prayer in which we ask God for guidance, *"...Remind me, Father, now, for I am weary of the world I see. Reveal what You would have me see instead."* The way to discover God's Will is to call upon the Holy Spirit or Jesus and to ask

---

[53] *ACIM*, W235.
[54] *ACIM*, M33.

Them for help in healing our split mind. Putting into practice the teachings of the Course will also help.

Lesson 272, *"How can illusions satisfy God's Son?"*[55] may be a helpful reminder that everything that we see with the body's eyes is an illusion. And if we are sincere about seeking the truth, how can we let illusions obscure the truth from us? This lesson asks us to turn away from any temptation to remain in our dream world, and to choose Heaven instead. On the other hand, there will probably always be things that we do enjoy in this world, and that's all right too. Listening to beautiful classical music can be an inspiring, spiritual experience. Walking in a forest or along the beach is also enjoyable and inspiring. As is watching young children play, communing with our pets and eating a tasty meal. Another pleasant experience is sitting in an English country garden on a warm, sunny summer's day whilst watching the birds. That has to be one of the nicest ways of relaxing. There is nothing wrong with enjoying the world of dreams for the time being provided we remember that it is just that—a dream world. There is no point in becoming saddened and embittered by the world whilst we still appear to be living in it.

One of the goals of *ACIM* is for us to reach the *"real world"* which, as we have seen before, is a world where everything is forgiven and which we look upon with Christ's vision. In Chapter 13 we are asked to, *"Sit quietly and look upon the world you see, and tell yourself: 'The real world is not like this. It has no buildings and there are no streets where people walk alone and separate. There are no stores where people buy an endless list of things they do not need. It is not lit with artificial light, and night comes not upon it. There is no day that brightens and grows dim. There is no loss. Nothing is there but shines, and shines forever."*[56] We are told that we cannot see or reach the real world if we are immersed in our illusory world. *"**You cannot see both worlds**, for each of them involves a different kind of seeing, and depends on what you cherish."* If we cherish the world that we look upon with our eyes, we will not escape from it. But if we value the goal of *ACIM* we will eventually be able to look upon the real

---

[55] *ACIM*, W432.

[56] *ACIM*, T254.

world with the vision of Christ. Our world of form was made out of fear (by projection from the split mind) but the real world will be attainable when we turn from fear to love. However, the world of form has to lose its appeal to us before we can reach the real world because, as just mentioned, *we cannot see both worlds*. So, we should rejoice if we find that we have become disillusioned with what this imaginary world has to offer. We are, after all, trying to overcome all illusions in our quest for the truth.

CHAPTER 16

HAVING LOW SELF-ESTEEM AND A LACK OF SELF-CONFIDENCE

Working in a school one comes across many pupils who suffer from low self-esteem and a lack of self-confidence. They are children who don't excel in what everybody else seems to excel in; they may be dyslexic and have difficulty with reading and spelling; or they may struggle with reading comprehension or with mathematics; they may be clumsy and have poor co-ordination and handwriting difficulties; they may be autistic and appear to live in a world of their own; or they may be children suffering from neglect or some other form of child abuse. What they all have in common is a feeling of being inferior to or different from their peers. This situation, which occurs in most schools, can also be found in the work-place. Yet, it doesn't have to be this way. It is a product of the values imposed upon us by the ego.

The list of things that can put us down is a long one; getting the sack, failing in exams at school, not passing our driving test, not being in a relationship, etc., are just a few examples. Yet, if we remember who we truly are, holy Sons of God, we would realize that there is no need to suffer from low self-esteem no matter what is going on in our lives. It doesn't matter if we "fail" at all the things that are considered important and worth valuing in this world – they are all illusions! It doesn't matter if I can't read very well, if I don't go to university, if I don't have a wonderful career, if I don't have a family, etc. It doesn't matter if we have no one to go on holiday with, or if we spend Christmas day alone, or if we have the most menial of jobs. Education, careers, making a lot of money, relationships, etc., are things that are only important to the ego. We have a much loftier goal, which is the salvation of the world, and the way to achieve that is to travel along the road of love and forgiveness.

Some people actually commit suicide if things go wrong in their lives, e.g., if they can't marry the person they love or if they lose all their money in a stock market crash—so sad! It's time we get our priorities right.   And when we finally realize that all the above-mentioned things are not that important, we begin to feel liberated. It's not easy because society drums into us the need for an education, a steady job, a family and a healthy bank balance. So it requires courage to let go, even a little, of the values we were brought up with and have been conditioned by.

What we have to remember is that the Course keeps insisting that the ego has created an insane world and that, if we want to achieve salvation, we need to embrace a new perception of the world. It asks us to completely overturn all the beliefs and values of the ego and to turn to the Holy Spirit for the truth. The thought system of the ego and that of the Holy Spirit are two opposing thought systems, and we can't combine the two. We read in the Workbook: *"To know reality is not to see the ego and its thoughts, its works, its acts, its laws and its beliefs, its dreams, its hopes, its plans for its salvation, and the cost belief in it entails."*[57] And in Lesson 32 we read: *"I have invented the world I see."* The world, being an invention, is, therefore, unreal; it makes no sense to worry about all the things this unreal world deems to be important.

Which lessons can we use to help us remember our true worth? We could start with Lesson 35: *"My mind is part of God's. I am very holy."* This is an extremely powerful and empowering statement. Lesson 35 goes on to explain: *"It is difficult for anyone who thinks he is in this world to believe this of himself. Yet the reason he thinks he is in this world is because he does not believe it."* We don't really believe that we are part of God. We see ourselves as separate, individual bodies, and we believe we need to compete with or, at least, keep up with other bodies. So, if other people have a good education, we believe we should. If everyone is able to buy their own home, we believe we should. Yet our true worth is not dependent on our qualifications or bank balance or the property we own. Our true worth depends on what is in our hearts and, above all, it comes from being part of God's mind. We can't fail at anything if we are really one with God.

Another important lesson to use when we are feeling bad about

---

[57] *ACIM,* W467.

ourselves is Lesson 299: *"Eternal holiness abides in me."* Jesus acknowledges that it is difficult for us to truly believe we are holy for he says in this lesson: *"My holiness is far beyond my own ability to understand or know. Yet God, my Father, Who created it, acknowledges my holiness as His..."* If eternal holiness abides in me, does it matter how much money I have in the bank? Does it matter if I can't read or write properly? Does it matter if I have a family or not?

Jesus does not have anything positive to say about the world of the ego and the beliefs of the ego. One cannot but agree with him as one looks around at the mess we have made of our dream world. The following passage was quoted before but it needs repeating because of its importance: *"Think of the freedom in the recognition that you are not bound by all the strange and twisted laws you have set up to save you. You really think that you would starve unless you have stacks of green paper strips and piles of metal discs. You really think a small round pellet or some fluid pushed into your veins through a sharpened needle will ward off disease and death. You really think you are alone unless another body is with you. It is insanity that thinks these things. You call them laws, and put them under different names in a long catalogue of rituals that have no use and serve no purpose..."*[58] Yet, it takes a lot of faith and courage to try to make do without a steady supply of *"green paper strips."*

It's not surprising we suffer from a lack of self-confidence and low self-esteem when we understand the dynamics of the ego. In the Workbook, Jesus describes our ego as, *"...a distorted image of yourself, confused, bewildered, inconsistent and unsure of everything..."*[59] It is worth reading Chapter 11, Section V of the Text, for further insights into the ego.

If ever we do have moments when our self-esteem is rather low, Lesson 186 should serve to remind us that we *are* important and that we have a vital function to fulfill. *"Salvation of the world depends on me."* Wow! Can I really help the world to awaken from its collective dream? And how can I be lacking in self-confidence if the salvation of the world depends on me? Explaining this lesson, Jesus says: *"...All it*

---

[58] *ACIM*, W134.

[59] *ACIM*, W353.

says is that your Father still remembers you, and offers you the perfect trust He holds in you who are His Son. It does not ask that you be different in any way from what you are. "[60] We also read in this lesson: *"If God's Voice assures you that salvation needs your part, and that the whole depends on you, be sure that it is so."* If we really have an important function to fulfill in God's plan, how can we suffer from low self-esteem?

It's important to remember that our function is forgiveness. If we are able to forgive we will awaken. Would it matter then what our bank balance was or if we had a successful career or not?

---

[60] *ACIM,* W351.

CHAPTER 17

FEELING FRIGHTENED ABOUT
WHAT LIES AHEAD

We live in times of great change and instability; world economies are struggling, climate change is causing great concern, and people around the world are rising up against their corrupt and brutal leaders. And, at a more personal level, people may suddenly find they have developed a serious illness; have an accident; be made redundant or lose a loved one. Nothing is predictable or safe in the illusory world of the ego. So it would seem natural to be apprehensive, if not frightened, about what the future may hold in store.

Yet, *A Course in Miracles* frequently reminds us that we have no reason to be afraid of anything because we are all holy Sons of God. Being like God, we have His strength. Everything we fear is related to our physical form but, if we remember that we are not our bodies, then we have nothing to fear. Whilst it's easy to understand this at the theoretical level, it is not easy to accept it whole-heartedly in practice.

So it's useful to turn to certain Workbook lessons for comfort and clarification. Lesson 240 is a good place to start: *"Fear is not justified in any form."* This lesson points out that if we feel afraid of anything it is because we have forgotten who we are. As holy Sons of God nothing can harm us. Furthermore, all the things we are afraid of don't even exist! *"Not one thing in this world is true."*[61] That is a strong statement which reminds us, yet again, that everything around us is an illusion.

It's not really surprising that we feel afraid at times since the Course tells us that our world is, actually, a symbol of fear. *"The world was made as an attack on God. It symbolizes fear. And what is fear except love's absence? Thus the world was meant to be a place God could enter not, and where His Son could be apart from Him."*[62]

---

[61] *ACIM,* W412.
[62] *ACIM,* W413.

But as this is not possible, because we are still one with God and with each other, then ACIM insists there is nothing to fear. When we awaken from a nightmare in the middle of the night, we are no longer afraid. When we awaken from our dream world, all fear will vanish.

Another lesson which spells out exactly why it is that we are safe is Lesson 244: *"I am in danger nowhere in the world"*. We are not in danger because God goes with us wherever we go, as we are a part of Him. And whilst, in our world, danger from one source or another may seem to be a real possibility, this cannot be, because we are not in this world, although it seems that we are. *"Your Son is safe wherever he may be, for You are there with him. He need but call upon Your Name, and he will recollect his safety and Your Love, for they are one."* [63]

Lesson 337: *"My sinlessness protects me from all harm"* is yet another lesson which reiterates that we cannot come to any harm. It tells us that all we need to do to be happy is to accept the Atonement. The reason we struggle with completely accepting this idea is because we have identified with the ego for lifetime after lifetime. Moreover, to really accept the Atonement and awaken, we are told that we must make God our only goal, as mentioned before. This is not easy as we are so caught up in our day-to-day lives, looking after our families, holding down a job, doing the shopping and cooking, etc., etc. Would awakening be any easier if we cut ourselves off from humanity and lived the life of a hermit in a cave? Maybe it would be, or maybe not. A life of isolation would not give us the forgiveness opportunities that our busy lives give us. But what we need to do as we go about our daily lives is to keep constantly aware that God is our only meaningful goal.

One can think of many instances in life when the future seems uncertain and we, naturally, become apprehensive; it happens to all of us. Losing a job, having a serious illness or facing retirement on a very low income are just examples of things that could arouse fear. There is no easy solution except to turn all problems over to the Holy Spirit and to call upon Him for guidance every single day when one gets up in the morning. Just as life dishes out unfortunate, even tragic, experiences from time to time, it also dishes out pleasant surprises.

---

[63] *ACIM,* W415.

Things may not turn out to be as bad we think they will. And even if they do, they may be learning experiences for us which will help us awaken. If life was a bed of roses, we would have no motivation to awaken.

Lesson 193, referred to in Chapter 14, states: *"All things are lessons God would have me learn."* This is an important lesson, which has the following key message: *"Forgive, and you will see this differently."* Jesus tells us that *"...all distress does not appear to be but unforgiveness"*—yet it is. The Holy Spirit asks us to forgive regardless of what is going on in our lives. *"These are the words the Holy Spirit speaks in all your tribulations, all your pain, all suffering regardless of its form. These are the words with which temptation ends, and guilt, abandoned, is revered no more. These are the words which end the dream of sin, and rid the mind of fear. These are the words by which salvation comes to all the world."*[64] It is clear from this passage that forgiveness will help us overcome fear but it takes a great deal of faith to accept this when we are in the midst of a crisis.

Lesson 46 tells us *"God is the Love in which I forgive."* It explains that love is the basis of forgiveness. *"Fear condemns and love forgives. Forgiveness thus undoes what fear has produced, returning the mind to the awareness of God. For this reason, forgiveness can truly be called salvation. It is the means by which illusions disappear."* And when our illusions disappear all our problems will automatically disappear too. When that time comes we will know that fear was not justified in any form.

Speaking in Hawaii in 2011, ACIM teacher David Hoffmeister said the ego mind is full of false concepts that cause us to be upset. The ego believes in lack and that's why we feel we have to work at a job to survive. But as we gradually allow the light of God into our lives, we will no longer identify with ego concepts. Eventually, as we move along with Spirit and as we empty our minds of all concepts and opinions, we will experience the light and will know who we really are. He says at this point we will realize that we are not sustained by money or food but we are sustained by the presence of love in our mind. Concepts like jobs will eventually be outgrown and we will find

---

[64] *ACIM,* W367.

that everything is taken care of effortlessly. David said it took him about 25 years to reach that point. We are lucky to have such an advanced teacher to show us the way and encourage us as we travel along the path to God.

CHAPTER 18

BEING TOO DISTRACTED BY DAILY ACTIVITIES TO THINK OF GOD

Lesson 64, *"Let me not forget my function,"* warns us about being distracted by the world. *"The purpose of the world you see is to obscure your function of forgiveness, and provide you with a justification for forgetting it. It is the temptation to abandon God and His Son by taking on a physical appearance."* It is very easy to become so absorbed in the distractions of the world that we forget our one and only meaningful function—awakening through forgiveness. In this lesson we are asked to affirm the following: *"Let me not forget my function. Let me not try to substitute mine for God's. Let me forgive and be happy."*

We try to substitute our own functions for God's every time we work towards a goal that we have set ourselves in this world. We could be working towards improving our education, working our way up the ladder at work or building up our bank balance. Whilst these things appear to be necessary in our world, we must make sure that we are not so preoccupied by them that we overlook our true function, which is forgiveness. We can actually pursue these goals and, at the same time, use our daily lives as the perfect setting to practice forgiveness. But it is important to remember that we really only have one goal.

On the other hand, we may devote all our time and energy to our earthly goals, and this will simply delay our awakening and could lead to further earthly lives, which, if we are serious about enlightenment, we should strive to avoid. We are told in the Text that the ego tries to make sure that we do not commit ourselves to anything that is eternal, because it has not been able to achieve eternalness in anything. The eternal can only come from God, and so the ego tries to keep our minds off this. *"The ego's characteristic busyness with nonessentials.... Preoccupations with problems set up to be incapable*

of solution are favorite ego devices for impeding learning progress."[65]
Jesus then tells us that we need to keep asking ourselves: *"What for?"*
We need to ask this question, *"in connection with everything."* What
are we doing this or that for? If we are doing it to help us in our
spiritual quest and in accordance with the teachings of *A Course in
Miracles* (or any other spiritual teaching we are following) then it
means we have not forgotten our true function.

On page 148 in the Text we are reminded that only the eternal is
worth striving for. *"No one created by God can find joy in anything
except the eternal; not because he is deprived of anything else, but
because nothing else is worthy of him. What God and His Sons create
is eternal, and in this and this only is Their joy."* All the goals we have
set ourselves and all the things we work and strive for will all come to
an end one day. It makes sense, therefore, to focus instead on the truth
and eternal peace.

Another very interesting point is raised in the section of the Text
entitled, *"The Body as Means or End."* Here it is pointed out that
whenever we achieve what we want, we don't remain satisfied for
long. *"...You must have noticed an outstanding characteristic of every
end that the ego has accepted as its own. When you have achieved it, **it
has not satisfied you.** This is why the ego is forced to shift ceaselessly
from one goal to another, so that you will continue to hope it can yet
offer you something."*[66] And this is why we move from one special
relationship to another; from one country to another; from one job to
another; from one holiday to another; from one house to another; from
one car to another and from one gadget to another.

According to Yogic philosophy, everything is governed by the
three gunas: sattva, rajas and tamas. Rajas makes our minds overactive
and keeps us very busy. Tamas, on the other hand, makes us lethargic
and lazy, whereas sattva is the perfect balance between these two
extremes, i.e., perfect harmony. Those who are influenced by too
much rajas or tamas are likely to have difficulty remembering their
true goal—God. Over-activity or excessive indolence are major
obstacles that can only be overcome by choosing a more sattvic

---

[65] *ACIM*, T67.
[66] *ACIM*, T155.

lifestyle. It is interesting to note that, according to the Yoga Sutras of Patanjali, when there is perfect equilibrium between the three gunas, *"There will be no manifestation of the universe."*[67] This is a very similar teaching to *A Course in Miracles*, which states that when we have all awakened to the truth and reached the real world, the world of form will simply disappear.

Which lessons can we use to help us to focus on God and to withdraw somewhat from the distractions of the world? Lesson 232, *"Be in my mind, my Father, through the day,"* is a good place to start. The prayer in this lesson is very beautiful and moving, and it is a wonderful way to start the day—every day. Another helpful lesson is Lesson 231, *"Father, I will but to remember You."* This lesson reinforces in our mind the fact that God is our only goal, even though we may seek other things. *"...Perhaps I think I seek for something else; a something I have called by many names. Yet is Your Love the only thing I seek, or ever sought...Let me remember You. What else could I desire but the truth about myself?"*

Memory is yet another ego tool that keeps us stuck in the world of the ego. *"Memory, like perception, is a skill made up by you to take the place of what God gave in your creation. And like all the things you made, it can be used to serve another purpose...It can be used to heal and not to hurt, if you so wish it be."*[68] The way to use our memory to heal is to listen to the Holy Spirit and to give others the miracle of love and forgiveness. *"The miracle but shows the past is gone and what has truly gone has no effects..."* This is because if we forgive someone it means we no longer hold anything against them and we are ready to move forward in our relationship with them.

The Holy Spirit uses memory to release time. How can this be done? By practicing forgiveness, by never holding a grudge against anyone and by never judging anyone. *"When ancient memories of hate appear, remember that their cause is gone...Be glad that it is gone, for this is what you would be pardoned from...What **you** remember never was. It came from causelessness which you confused with cause...The miracle reminds you of a Cause forever present, perfectly untouched*

---

[67] http://swamij.com/yoga-sutras-41314.htm
[68] *ACIM*, T589.

by time and interference. Never changed from what It is. And you are Its Effect, as changeless and as perfect as Itself..."[69] The Cause referred to here is God.

As pointed out before, if we are busy rushing around all day long it will be difficult for miracles to enter into our lives, unless we make a point of being loving, forgiving and kind whist we are doing this. But we really need to have moments of stillness and quiet every day when we can empty the mind of all the clutter of the ego. Jesus asks us to use our memory to remember God and to remember our oneness with Him and all of His creation. This contrasts with the ego's use of memory, which makes sure we **don't** remember God by keeping us fixated on the *"figures in the dream"* (other people) and what they may have done to upset us or harm us. The ego will do all it can to prevent us from forgiving others, because if we forgive and forget we will be more likely to remember our oneness with God.

Meditation has been dealt with previously in this book, but it is worth reiterating that regular meditation is a good way to try to shut out the clamor of the ego. A few minutes of meditation first thing in the morning is a wonderful way to greet the day. It is also possible, when we are at work, to stop for just a minute, every so often, and remember God. One could just stop what one is doing, close one's eyes and repeat any of these lessons: *"Let me remember that my goal is God." "Peace to my mind. Let all my thoughts be still." "In quiet I receive God's Word today." "I want the peace of God." "Let every voice but God's be still in me."*[70] In Lesson 258 Jesus gives us this advice: *"All that is needful is to train our minds to overlook all little senseless aims, and to remember that our goal is God. His memory is hidden in our minds, obscured but by our pointless little goals which offer nothing, and do not exist."*

---

[69] *ACIM,* T590 & T591.
[70] *ACIM,* Lessons 258, 221, 125, 185, 254.

CHAPTER 19

JUDGING SOMEONE WHO HAS DONE SOMETHING WRONG

Whether we realize it or not, we make judgments about people and events all the time; it seems to be human nature to judge others. We judge when someone says something upsetting; we judge when we watch the television news or read the newspapers; we judge when we side with a political party—believing that the party we support is superior to others; we judge people who have different religious beliefs from ourselves. We also judge a person as soon as he walks into the room; he could be too tall, too short, too old, too ugly, badly-dressed, etc. It has been said that the first few minutes of a job interview are the most important. This is probably because the interviewer is sizing up the interviewee based on his appearance, his demeanor and his body language. Physical appearances *are* of importance to the ego but we have to learn to look beyond them in our endeavor to rise above the world of form.

In judging people and events and in taking sides, we build barriers between "us" and "them", and these barriers will: *"...bind my eyes and make me blind."*[71] If we pick up any newspaper and read the headlines we will realize that nothing could be more judgmental. In fact, journalists would have very little to write about if they were told to eliminate all judgment and finger-pointing from their writing.

The *ACIM* teacher Kenneth Wapnick deals with this issue in his book, *Ending our Resistance to Love*. *"Watch the news and see how your buttons get pushed. You will hate and judge some people, and perceive others as the 'good guys'....when your point of view starts to exclude others, and you feel personal antipathy toward certain people or groups, that should indicate you are still afraid of God's Love."*[72]

---

[71] *ACIM*, W480.

[72] Kenneth Wapnick, Ph.D., *Ending our Resistance to Love*, p. 55, *Foundation for A Course in Miracles*, Temecula, CA, 2004.

Jesus tells us that it is meaningless to judge one another. *"You have no idea of the tremendous release and deep peace that comes from meeting yourself and your brothers totally without judgment. When you recognize what you are and what your brothers are, you will realize that judging them in any way is without meaning."*[73] Judgment is meaningless because we are all one; thus in judging another we judge ourselves. Moreover, we are judging words spoken and deeds performed in a dream and not in reality. What point is there in judging figures in a dream?

Not only is judgment meaningless, it brings with it, *"all the sorrows of the world."* One example that springs to mind is war. Wars are waged because one country judges another and feels the need to change that country in some way. Or it may want to obtain a scarce resource from it; so it starts a war. And what can be more sorrowful than war?

We are not in a position to judge another because we don't know all the ins and outs of the situation. It could be that someone made an upsetting remark about another or it could be more serious like theft or even murder. Regardless of the offence, we cannot judge fairly because: *"In order to judge anything rightly, one would have to be fully aware of an inconceivably wide range of things; past, present and to come. One would have to recognize in advance all the effects of his judgments on everyone and everything involved in them in any way. And one would have to be certain there is no distortion in his perception, so that his judgment would be wholly fair to everyone on whom it rests now and in the future. Who is in a position to do this?"*[74]

There are a number of lessons that serve as useful reminders when we notice we are just about to judge a person, a group of people or an event. Lesson 259 reminds us, *"Let me remember that there is no sin"* and Lesson 335 asserts, *"I choose to see my brother's sinlessness."* This lesson points out that we are projecting our thoughts onto others, *"...What I see in him is merely what I wish to see, because it stands for what I want to be the truth."* It is explained in this lesson that if we choose to forgive someone this will restore the memory of God to us—

---

[73] *ACIM*, T47.
[74] *ACIM*, M27.

amazing!

Projection is a typical characteristic of the ego. It projects its own thoughts and feelings onto others to make it feel better about itself. If one comes across, for example, an angry driver, it could be that one has created this driver because one still has one's own anger issues to deal with. The angry driver is just reflecting back the contents of one's mind. *"The secret of salvation is but this: that you are doing this unto yourself. No matter what the form of the attack, this still is true...And you will understand that miracles reflect the simple statement, 'I have done this thing, and it is this I would undo'... "*[75] The sensible thing to do in such a situation is to realize that one has to work at transmuting one's own anger into peace. This realization will make it easy to forgive the driver for his anger and to put the incident out of one's mind.

Another Lesson we could use whenever we feel tempted to judge someone is Lesson 243: *"Today I will judge nothing that occurs."* This is excellent advice because, *"...I will not think I understand the whole from bits of my perception, which are all that I can see."* Because we don't have the whole picture, we are not in a position to judge. We don't know what is going on in the mind of a certain offender or in his life, or what happened in his previous lifetimes, and so we can't judge him fairly. And, above all, we need to remember that this life is just a dream. We are all dreaming that we are here on earth, living our lives separate from each other and separate from God. In one of the most well-known passages of *A Course in Miracles* Jesus states, *"You are at home in God, dreaming of exile but perfectly capable of awakening to reality."*[76]

Whenever a crime has been committed it is helpful to remember that it is the *ego* of the perpetrator which is responsible, but not the man himself because, as mentioned before, we are all holy Sons of God. *"My holy Self abides in you, God's Son."*[77] This statement is applicable to *all* humanity.

The Course continually reminds us that we cannot get to Heaven

---

[75] *ACIM,* T587.
[76] *ACIM,* T182.
[77] *ACIM,* W428.

on our own; we need to take others there with us by forgiving them. In this way they become our saviors. In Lesson 288, *"Let me forget my brother's past today,"* we are reminded that our brother's sins are in the past, as are our own sins. And with reference to our inherent equality with each other and with Jesus, we read, *"Forgive me, then, today. And you will know you have forgiven me if you behold your brother in the light of holiness. He cannot be less holy than can I, and you can not be holier than he."*[78]

One further lesson we can use to help us rise above the temptation to judge another person or group of people is Lesson 352:

"Judgment and love are opposites. From one
Come all the sorrows of the world. But from
The other comes the peace of God Himself."

What more could we desire than the peace of God?

---

[78] *ACIM,* W441.

CHAPTER 20

FEELING DIFFERENT FROM OTHERS

Egalitarianism is at the heart of the teachings of *A Course in Miracles*. Jesus tells us that no one is different from anyone else and neither are we different from him. We are *all* holy Sons of God. This sentence, quoted in the previous chapter, is evidence of this belief: *"...He cannot be less holy than can I, and you can not be holier than he.* "[79] We are all one.

Yet, our society does not treat everyone as equals. If a person has a college degree he may be judged to be a better person than the man who sweeps the street. The director of a company is held in greater esteem than is the person who cleans his office. A successful businessman is deemed to be superior to the homeless drunk who sits on the pavement. There are endless examples of just how different we are from each other. But if all that is going on in our world is just a dream, then surely it makes no difference what we do? In one lifetime I could have a dream of being a successful career woman and in the next lifetime I could dream that I am an impoverished tramp. The only thing that really matters is whether or not I am able to awaken from the dream world altogether.

All comparisons are ego-based. The ego goes out of its way to try to compare itself to others and to feel superior to others; this is part of its dynamics. As we have seen, it projects all its inadequacies onto others so that it can feel better about itself. If we are tempted to compare ourselves to another person or to feel superior to another in some way, it is helpful to recall Lesson 164: *"Now are we one with Him who is our Source."* If we are all one with God then we must be one with each other. Therefore, no one is better or worse than anyone else.

---

[79] *ACIM,* W441.

Lesson 181: *"I trust my brothers, who are one with me,"* underpins our essential unity with each other. Everyone I see is *"one with me."* If they are one with me, how could it be possible for me to judge them as being worse than me in any way? Lesson 243: *"Today I will judge nothing that occurs,"* also states unequivocally that we are all one: *"...We are one because each part contains Your memory, and truth must shine in all of us as one."*[80]

In the section entitled *"What am I?"* in the Workbook we are told that we are *"...God's Son, complete and healed and whole..."* Moreover, *"We look on everyone as brother, and perceive all things as kindly and as good..."*[81] Earlier on in the Workbook there is a beautiful definition of oneness: *"Oneness is simply the idea God is. And in His Being, He encompasses all things. No mind holds anything but Him. We Say, 'God is,' and then we cease to speak, for in that knowledge words are meaningless..."*[82] If no mind holds anything but God, then it follows that all minds are joined and all minds are one.

"The Oneness of the Creator and the creation is your wholeness, your sanity and your limitless power. This limitless power is God's gift to you, because it is what you are. If you dissociate your mind from it you are perceiving the most powerful force in the universe as if it were weak, because you do not believe you are part of it."[83] This is an important passage because it shows us how foolish we are to deny our oneness with God and with each other; in doing so we are denying ourselves access to *"the most powerful force in the universe."* If we can truly accept Jesus' teachings about our oneness, then we will never again feel superior to anyone else on the planet. We are not even superior to the most crazed, criminal who goes on a mass killing rampage!

If there are times when we start to doubt our oneness with others, whether a particular person or a group of people, it would serve us well to read Lesson 95, *"I am one Self, united with my Creator."* This lesson explains that if we deny our oneness with God then we will

---

[80] *ACIM*, W415.
[81] *ACIM*, W479.
[82] *ACIM*, W323.
[83] *ACIM*, T125.

perceive ourselves as weak and sinful, but this is just an illusion for, *"You are one Self, the holy Son of God, united with your brothers in that Self; united with your Father in His Will."*[84] This belief is one of the cornerstones of *A Course in Miracles*. It is something we have to tell ourselves over and over again if we wish to master the teachings of the Course. And whenever a situation arises in which we start to compare ourselves with others or start to feel superior to someone else, for whatever reason, then the best thing is to look at the person and mentally tell him: *"You are one Self with me, united with our Creator in this Self. I honor you because of What I am, and What He is, Who loves us both as One."*[85]

---

[84] *ACIM,* W168.
[85] *ACIM,* W168.

CHAPTER 21

WHEN RESPONDING TO A DIFFICULT PERSON OR SITUATION

There will be times in life when we come across a person who seems antagonistic, and situations which seem challenging. Even if we leave our current job and move on to another one, sure enough a difficult person or situation will reappear in our new place of work. There is a reason for this; there are forgiveness lessons we still have to learn. Lesson 193 tells us: *"All things are lessons God would have me learn."* Although we may find certain things to be difficult and challenging, *"God sees no contradictions."* Therefore, we need His help to correct the errors in our minds. *"Forgive, and you will see this differently,"* is the advice given in this lesson.

After all, it is only because of the initial erroneous decision of our split mind that we find ourselves here on earth. The correction of the errors in our minds is what *A Course in Miracles* is all about. In an important section of Chapter 18 of the Manual for Teachers we read, *"...If he senses even the faintest hint of irritation in himself as he responds to anyone, let him instantly realize that he has made an interpretation that is not true. Then let him turn within to his eternal Guide, and let Him judge what the response should be. So is he healed, and in his healing is his pupil healed with him."*[86] Most of us feel the faintest hint of irritation quite often during our daily lives. It could be annoyance about having to do the washing up or put the rubbish out; it could be irritation due to having to attend a boring meeting at work; it could be frustration because the computer has frozen, etc. Whatever the situation, we need to remember that annoyance, irritation or anger are not justified because these feelings make our perceived problems seem real. We wouldn't become annoyed by an irritating person or situation in a dream we have at night. Yet our daytime experiences are as unreal as our nighttime dreams. The solution is to accept the

---

[86] *ACIM*, M48.

difficult person or situation with a smile and to tell ourselves, *"All things are lessons God would have me learn."* It would also help if we remembered that it is only the ego or wrong portion of the split mind that is irritated because the right portion of the mind is always peaceful and serene, as that is where the Holy Spirit dwells.

We actually *invite* difficult people and circumstances into our lives either to help us learn the lessons we need to learn or because we have anger and irritation within our own minds which we project outwards. The following quotation, which was mentioned in Chapter 19, spells this out: *"The secret of salvation is but this: that you are doing this unto yourself. No matter what the form of the attack, this still is true..."* Until we realize that we are the cause of our own problems and suffering, we will find ourselves faced with challenging situations. *"...The Holy Spirit will repeat this one inclusive lesson of deliverance until it has been learned, regardless of the form of suffering that brings you pain. Whatever hurt you bring to Him He will make answer with this very simple truth. For this one answer takes away the cause of every form of sorrow and of pain..."* What is the answer? *"'I have done this thing, and it is this I would undo.'"*[87] In other words, we have to take complete responsibility for all that we seem to be experiencing in our lives.

One way to do this is to study Lesson 23, *"I can escape from the world I see by giving up attack thoughts."* The following passage explains why we need to take responsibility for our thoughts. *"If the cause of the world you see is attack thoughts, you must learn that it is these thoughts which you do not want."*[88] The world is simply the result or the effect of our thoughts; peaceful thoughts will produce a peaceful world.

One of the lessons which can help us in difficult times is Lesson 243, *"Today I will judge nothing that occurs."* As we have already seen, this lesson tells us that we cannot see the whole picture in any situation and so we are not in a position to judge anything. In accepting this, we experience peace. *"...Thus do I free myself and what*

---

[87] *ACIM,* T588.
[88] *ACIM,* W34.

I look upon, to be in peace as God created us. "[89] Therefore, it makes sense if one is stuck in a boring meeting or in a traffic jam or in a long, slow queue to accept the situation and remember that we are in it for a reason. We could use the time wisely by mentally repeating certain Course lessons which bring us peace and joy. Some of these will be discussed in the last chapter.

"Forgiveness ends the dream of conflict here,"[90] is a lesson which can be used in many different situations. Lesson 333 contains the essence of the complete teachings of *A Course in Miracles.* It depicts the ego's world of duality as a world of conflict, but it reminds us that this is only a dream. And it tells us that forgiveness is the way to bring to an end the ego's illusory world and awaken from the dream. And there we have a succinct summary of the Course. *"Conflict must be resolved. It cannot be evaded, set aside, denied, disguised, seen somewhere else, called by another name, or hidden by deceit of any kind, if it would be escaped..."* The way to escape conflict is through forgiveness which is, *"...the light You chose to shine away all conflict and all doubt, and light the way for our return to You. No light but this can end our evil dream."* Note that the term *evil* in this passage simply means erroneous.

How can we find a way which will lead us out of suffering altogether? How can we ensure that we won't find ourselves in the position of having to put up with challenging people or situations? The answer can be summed up very easily in these three words: seek the truth. This is the message of Lesson 107, *"Truth will correct all errors in my mind."* Remember it is our minds that we are trying to change and not the circumstances in which we find ourselves because the latter are simply the result or the effect of what is going on in our minds. *"...When truth has come all pain is over, for there is no room for transitory thoughts and dead ideas to linger in your mind. Truth occupies your mind completely, liberating you from all beliefs in the ephemeral....Give truth its due, and it will give you yours. You were not meant to suffer and to die. Your Father wills these dreams be gone.*

---

[89] *ACIM,* W415.
[90] *ACIM,* W469.

Let truth correct them all."[91]

How do we find the truth? As stated before, we call upon the Holy Spirit to be our guide. A good way to do this is to invite Him into our lives first thing in the morning. As we saw in Chapter 18, we could call upon Him by reciting the prayer in Lesson 232, *"Be in my mind, my Father through the day."* It is also important to remember to call upon Him during the day whenever we find ourselves beginning to experience the *"faintest hint of irritation."* And the best thing we can do to hasten our journey Home is to forgive, forgive and forgive again.

---

[91] *ACIM,* W193.

CHAPTER 22

FEELING GUILTY

Guilt is at the root of all our problems in this world of illusions. As we have already seen and as is explained numerous times in *ACIM*, guilt stems from that initial moment of separation when the mind split in two and the ego came into being. The way the ego deals with guilt is to project it outside itself onto others; now it can blame others instead of itself. This, of course, justifies its feelings of anger at what it is experiencing at the hands of its enemies. It also justifies its defensiveness. Thus we have an endless cycle of guilt, projection, anger, attack and defense: the more we project our guilt and fear onto others, the angrier we get and, therefore, the more we attack them, which, in turn, creates more guilt. This has been repeated over and over again in all our lives ever since the perceived separation from God.

The following passage gives an important explanation about the link between the ego and guilt: *"...If the ego is the symbol of the separation, it is also the symbol of guilt. Guilt is more than merely not of God. It is the symbol of attack on God. This is a totally meaningless concept except to the ego, but do not underestimate the power of the ego's belief in it. This is the belief from which all guilt really stems."*[92] All the guilt we experience in our daily lives stems from this belief— both unconscious and conscious guilt. The problem we have is that we identify with the ego and are unaware that this world is not real and was not created by God. *"...The ego believes that this is what you did because it believes that it **is** you. If you identify with the ego, you must perceive yourself as guilty...Listening to the ego's voice means that you believe it is possible to attack God, and that a part of him has been torn away by you. Fear of retaliation from without follows, because the severity of the guilt is so acute that it must be projected."* The last sentence in this passage makes it clear why we feel the need to project

---

[92] *ACIM*, T84.

our guilt outside ourselves.

Projection of guilt means we will all experience difficult situations and difficult people in our lives, which, at some level, we have created ourselves. But if we can accept the Atonement, we have a way of overcoming this seemingly insurmountable problem. In acknowledging the Atonement, we become lucid dreamers, i.e., we recognize that this world is just a dream and we realize that we are both the dreamer and the dream.

There will be many occasions in our lives when we do feel guilty and also when other people make us feel guilty. But we have to stand firm and remember that we are sinless. *ACIM* tells us this over and over again. A good lesson to use to help us overcome guilt is Lesson 35, *"My mind is part of God's. I am very holy."* As the ego is the symbol of guilt and we, as spiritual seekers, are determined to overcome the ego, then we must make sure we are able to rise above guilty feelings. If not, we will remain imprisoned in this dream world by our guilt. Moreover, we must never make others feel guilty. It is very easy to blame someone who has done something we perceive to be wrong or hurtful, but if we can stop ourselves from blaming them we will be making good progress with the teachings of the Course. It may help if we remind ourselves that *we* have put those people and situations into our lives, and so it is pointless to blame them.

Lesson 190: *"I choose the joy of God instead of pain,"* serves as a useful reminder that we can control our feelings because we can choose them. *"It is your thoughts alone that cause you pain. Nothing external to your mind can hurt or injure you in any way...No one but yourself affects you. There is nothing in the world that has the power to make you ill or sad, or weak or frail. But it is you who have the power to dominate all things you see by merely recognizing what you are."*[93] Can we really recognize that we are holy Sons of God, sinless and immortal? That is one of the messages of *ACIM*.

Is the Course asking us not to feel guilty about *anything* we do, including committing a crime? No. *ACIM* is not concerned with all that is going on in the dream world. It is simply trying to teach us not to identify with the ego, and to turn instead to the Holy Spirit in our

---

[93] *ACIM,* W361.

minds, who teaches us that we are guiltless because we have never separated from God. *"As you look upon yourself and judge what you do honestly, you may be tempted to wonder how you can be guiltless. Yet consider this: You are not guiltless in time, but in eternity. You have "sinned" in the past, but there is no past. Always has no direction. Time seems to go in one direction, but when you reach its end it will roll up like a long carpet spread along the past behind you, and will disappear..."*[94] We have sinned in our dream world, and we sinned at the time of the separation but, as the separation never took place, the world of time and space is not real, so we remain guiltless *"in eternity."* When we accept the Atonement and return in our awareness to our pre-separation state, we are told that we will realize that there is no past or future—just the eternal now. Hence the reference above to time rolling up like a long carpet and disappearing. Time will disappear and the world will disappear. This is stated clearly at the end of Chapter 27 of the Text: *"...When you forgive the world your guilt, you will be free of it..."*[95]

If we feel guilty, it is because we believe we really committed a sin in the past by separating from God, and so we deserve to be punished for this in the future. In order to step out of time altogether we have to let go of all our guilty feelings and remember that we have not sinned and we have not left Heaven. If the thought of time ending arouses fear in us, it is because we are identifying with the body—the home of the ego. This fear is understandable but, if time doesn't end, we will be doomed to eternal cycles of life, death and rebirth in this dream world, which is not a very pleasant thought. So awakening from the dream, which will lead to the disappearance of the world of time and space, is the only goal that makes sense. To achieve it, we have to remember that, in the grand scheme of things, we have done nothing wrong.

It is helpful to remember these words: *"Son of God you have not sinned, but you have been much mistaken. Yet this can be corrected and God will help you, knowing that you could not sin against Him."*[96]

---

[94] *ACIM,* T237.

[95] *ACIM,* T588.

[96] *ACIM,* T190.

How can we perceive a murderer to be guiltless? In our dream world we can't, but we need to remember that it is only the *ego* of the murderer who has sinned and not the eternal, holy part of his split mind. The same applies to ourselves when we do something that pricks our conscience. *"When you feel guilty, remember that the ego has indeed violated the laws of God, but **you** have not. Leave the 'sins' of the ego to me. That is what Atonement is for. But until you change your mind about those whom your ego has hurt, the Atonement cannot release you. While you feel guilty your ego is in command, because only the ego can experience guilt. **This need not be.**"*[97] And in that passage we have an excellent reason why we must rise above guilt in one way or another; the best way is through forgiveness. We have to forgive ourselves for all the things we believe we have done wrong in our lives, and we have to forgive others for whatever crimes they may have committed. Remember *"only the ego can experience guilt."* This means each time we feel guilty we are identifying with the ego.

In Section VI of Chapter 30 entitled *The Justification for Forgiveness*, it is explained why forgiveness is *always* justified. The following quotation, which was mentioned earlier on in this book, shows why: *"You are not asked to offer pardon where attack is due, and would be justified. For that would mean that you forgive a sin by overlooking what is really there. This is not pardon...Salvation does not lie in being asked to make unnatural responses which are inappropriate to what is real. Instead, it merely asks that you respond appropriately to what is not real by not perceiving what has not occurred."*[98] Now that's an interesting justification for forgiveness and a completely different one from the traditional view of forgiveness in which we *are* asked to overlook the very real sins of others. Perhaps we should read the last part of the last sentence again. We are asked not to react to what is not real by, *"not perceiving what has not occurred."* A more straightforward way of putting this is given in the Workbook and was mentioned in Chapter 13: *"Forgiveness recognizes what you thought your brother did to you has not occurred. It does not pardon sins and make them real. It sees there was no sin. And in that*

---

[97] *ACIM,* T63.
[98] *ACIM,* T638.

view are all your sins forgiven."[99] This also applies to ourselves; we forgive ourselves for any misdemeanors *because they haven't actually happened.*

Lesson 156 is a helpful lesson to use if ever we feel guilty. *"I walk with God in perfect holiness."* This lesson stresses that there is no cause for guilt because we are not apart from God, *"...ideas leave not their source. If this be true, how can you be apart from God?"* We are an idea in the Mind of God and as *"ideas leave not their source,"* then we must still be in the Mind of God at this very moment; we are just dreaming that we are not.

If ever we doubt our guiltlessness we are told in Lesson 156 to remember: *"I walk with God in perfect holiness. I light the world, I light my mind and all the minds which God created one with me."*

---

[99] *ACIM,* W401.

CHAPTER 23

FEELING SAD AND UPSET BECAUSE OF ALL THE CRUELTY IN THE WORLD

There is no doubt that there are a lot of horrible things going on in the world. Some of us seem capable of unspeakable cruelty to others. We are also capable of inflicting great suffering upon the animal kingdom, and we aren't always too careful about the plant kingdom either. Without going into the dreadful detail of it all, suffice it to say that certain events and deeds can be really shocking and disturbing. Some people no longer watch the news on television or read the newspapers at all because of all the suffering they will be confronted with.

What does *A Course in Miracles*, tell us about the world? A great deal! Our world, we are told, is not our natural environment; we are like a fish out of water. It is, therefore, not surprising that things here get us down. *"...The world goes against your nature, being out of accord with God's laws...A Son of God is happy only when he knows he is with God. That is the only environment in which he will not experience strain, because that is where he belongs..."*[100]

Several lessons in the Workbook deal with the fact that our world is meaningless. As we saw earlier on in this book, Lesson 14 states: *"God did not create a meaningless world."* That is a good thing to remind oneself, when one perceives the horrors of the world. The reason why it is meaningless is because: *"What God did not create does not exist. And everything that does exist exists as He created it. The world you see has nothing to do with reality. It is of your own making, and it does not exist."*[101] Although it is difficult not to get upset by the natural disasters of the world, the crimes that are committed and the cruelty that is inflicted upon people and animals, it is helpful to remember that all this is *not real*.

---

[100] *ACIM*, T136.
[101] *ACIM*, W23.

The problem is that all the disasters, crimes and tragedies that unfold here seem very real. When this is the case, we can turn to Lesson 12: *"I am upset because I see a meaningless world,"* and, as we look around the world and notice what is going on, we are advised to say to ourselves: *"I think I see a fearful world, a dangerous world, a hostile world, a sad world, a wicked world, a crazy world...But I am upset because I see a meaningless world."*[102] It really doesn't make much sense to let a meaningless, non-existent world disturb our peace of mind. But what do we do when we are bombarded by the news of tragic events every single day of the year? Switch channels. Turn the news off and turn a music channel on instead, preferably the sort of music that brings you peace and puts a smile on your face. The only way to remain immune to the messages of the media is to become a bit like an ostrich.

The Course also points out that our world is insane. *"...It must be so that either God is mad, or is this world a place of madness. Not one Thought of His makes any sense at all within this world. And nothing that the world believes as true has any meaning in His Mind at all. What makes no sense and has no meaning is insanity. And what is madness cannot be truth..."*[103] So, truth-seekers don't waste your time trying to find any meaning in this world; don't fight for any cause that appears to benefit the world; don't do anything except focus on spreading the truth and awakening from the dream. When we have all awakened there will no longer be a world; it will simply disappear into oblivion. But we need to remember that, according to the Course, the way to awaken is to be forgiving and loving. Consequently, we do need to be kind and offer help when we can and to whom we can, but it is important to make sure we are not drawn into the dramas and tragedies of those whose paths we cross.

"Accepting the Atonement for yourself means not to give support to someone's dream of sickness and of death. It means that you share not his wish to separate, and let him turn illusions on himself...Refuse to be a part of fearful dreams whatever form they take, for you will lose identity in them....You stand apart from them, but not apart from

---

[102] *ACIM*, W19.
[103] *ACIM*, T531.

him who dreams them. Thus you separate the dreamer from the dream, and join in one, but let the other go. "[104] The last part of this passage is extremely important because it tells us not to get drawn into the problems of others but it also tells us not to stand apart from them; we mustn't abandon the dreamer because of his unhappy dreams.

Further on in the Text we are reminded, *"Remember if you share an evil dream, you will believe you are the dream you share. And fearing it, you will not want to know your own Identity, because you think that It is fearful. And you will deny your Self, and walk upon an alien ground which your Creator did not make, and where you seem to be a something you are not."*[105] This passage says a great deal. Firstly, by referring to our world as an *"evil dream"* it reminds us that it is just dream; and, secondly, it warns us that we will immerse ourselves in illusions if we share these dreams, because they will cause us to forget Who we really are.

We can do our friends and family members a favor by not dwelling on our own problems when we meet them or chat to them on the phone. Sometimes this won't be possible because it is natural to want to share our troubles with those who are close to us. But we could try to remember not to go on and on about our problems and not to complain about the sad events of the world, because it's best not to force our illusions on others.

A good lesson to use when our world makes us feel sad, angry or depressed is Lesson 23: *"I can escape from the world I see by giving up attack thoughts."* It was the *attack thoughts* of the ego which made this world in the first place. By accepting the Atonement (which is how we abandon our attack thoughts) we can reach the state in which we will be ready to live in the real world, which is a stone's throw away from Heaven, we are told.

As we saw in Chapter 21, Lesson 23 explains that it is pointless to try to change the world because it is an effect. We need to remind ourselves frequently that what we need to change is our perception of the world (the cause). It is essential to remember that we are the *"image maker"* who caused this world to come into being. When we

---

[104] *ACIM*, T598.
[105] *ACIM*, T601.

all become aware that we are one with each other, cruelty will come to an end because we will extend love and forgiveness to each other instead of projecting the ego's anger and guilt onto others as we do now. *Then* we will see a difference in our world—it will no longer be a world of chaos, cruelty and conflict.

That is the message of Lesson 301: *"And God Himself shall wipe away all tears."* In the prayer in this lesson we call upon God to help us change our perception of the world. *"...Let me today behold it uncondemned, through happy eyes forgiveness has released from all distortion. Let me see Your world instead of mine. And all the tears I shed will be forgotten, for their source is gone..."*[106] So, as we look around our world and notice how fearful, tragic and sad it is, we can quietly remind ourselves that *"God Himself shall wipe away all tears,"* when we no longer judge the world but offer it forgiveness instead because we recognize that it has no reality.

We need to forgive the world its limitations because its source is imperfect (the wrong mind). We need to forgive the limitations of everyone in the world, especially those who hurt us. We also need to forgive ourselves for our own limitations and for having listened to the ego and, as a result, being here in the world of form. It is important to realize that all limitations are unreal—just *"shadows"* as they are called in the Course. We should accept these limitations as learning experiences enabling us to choose again (the Holy Spirit instead of the ego). We look upon the limitations of the world with forgiveness and non-judgment because we made the world up, *"And nothing that you think you see in it is really there at all."*[107]

"The light of the world brings peace to every mind through my forgiveness," states Lesson 63. When I fulfill my function, which is forgiveness, not only will it bring me peace but it will also help spread peace around the world. When that happens we can expect to see a much nicer world than the one we see today. *"...You are indeed the light of the world with such a function...Accept no trivial purpose or meaningless desire in its place, or you will forget your function and*

---

[106] *ACIM*, W450.
[107] *ACIM*, T530.

leave the Son of God in hell. "[108] The message of this lesson is that we have to focus on healing our own minds through love and forgiveness; this will help heal the minds of others since all minds are joined. The ultimate result will be a healed world.

Reference was made earlier in this chapter to the need to be rather like an ostrich. Does this mean that we do not lend a helping hand to those in need? It definitely does not. Each of us has the right to help alleviate suffering in this dream world by whatever means we feel drawn to. The Course is not asking us to stop giving to charities or working in soup kitchens or doing other good deeds that help the poor, the sick and the homeless. But it stresses the most important thing we can do is to *heal our minds* through love and forgiveness. Indeed, those who are loving and forgiving will automatically extend their love to others in whatever way they can. Yet, it is not the money we give to the poor or the help that we give to those in need that will make this world a better place for the simple reason that the world can never become a better place *because it does not really exist*—it is simply the effect of what is in our minds. Remember Lesson 32: *"I have invented the world I see."* By healing our minds, we heal the *cause* of all the problems in the world. That *will* make a difference.

The following passage, in which Jesus speaks to us, clarifies this issue: *"...We walk together. I must understand uncertainty and pain, although I know they have no meaning. Yet a savior must remain with those he teaches, seeing what they see, but still retaining in his mind the way that led him out, and now will lead you out with him... I am renewed each time a brother learns there is a way from misery and from pain..."* This shows that Jesus recognizes that there is uncertainty, misery and pain in our world but he is asking us to remember that *"they have no meaning."* He is asking us, instead, to turn towards the light by being forgiving. This does not mean that we ignore the rest of humanity who appear to be suffering. But Jesus is telling us that the only thing we can do to really help others is to lead them, as well as ourselves, to the light. *"...Take your brother's hand, for this is not a way we walk alone. In him I walk with you, and you*

---

[108] *ACIM*, W105.

with me... "[109]

We don't abandon the world to its misery; we help the world to awaken from the dream by passing on the message of *A Course in Miracles: "You are my voice, my eyes, my feet, my hands through which I save the world."* This is more crucial than helping to solve the myriad of problems that we are faced with in all corners of the globe.

---

[109] *ACIM,* W330.

CHAPTER 24

FEELING UNFAIRLY TREATED BY SOMEONE OR BY CIRCUMSTANCES

Someone misjudges you and makes a hurtful comment; someone barges in front of you in the supermarket to get to the check-out before you; someone swears at you as you are driving along in your car; someone gossips about you behind your back; you go for a job interview but, despite you qualifications and skills, you don't get the job; a pile of paperwork is dumped on your desk on a Friday afternoon; you live a healthy lifestyle but suddenly succumb to a serious illness. Those are just a few illustrations of occasions when we would, understandably, feel that we had been treated unfairly. Yet, *A Course in Miracles* tells us otherwise.

ACIM insists that none of us are victims of what is going on in our lives or in the world. As we have seen, it asks us to take full and total responsibility for everything we experience because we have projected our thoughts out into the world and onto other people; these thoughts are then reflected back to us in the form of our experiences.

"I am not a victim of the world I see," states Lesson 31. *"I have invented the world I see,"* asserts Lesson 32. *"You are not a victim of the world you see because you invented it. You can give it up as easily as you made it up. You will see it or not see it, as you wish. While you want it you will see it; when you no longer want it, it will not be there for you to see."*[110] We see the world because the ego projected it outwards; it is a mental image, which reflects our state of mind. As the ego mind is deluded, fearful and full of guilt, we cannot really expect to have a peaceful and happy existence until we begin to detach from the ego and start to heal our split minds. Guilt is particularly injurious because if it is projected inwards it can cause ill health; if it is projected outwards it creates enemies.

"The world you see depicts exactly what you thought you did.

---

[110] *ACIM*, W49.

*Except that now you think that what you did is being done to you. The guilt for what you thought is being placed outside yourself, and on a guilty world that dreams your dreams and thinks your thoughts instead of you. It brings a vengeance, not your own...The world but demonstrates an ancient truth; you will believe that others do to you exactly what you think you did to them. But once deluded into blaming them you will not see the cause of what they do, because you **want** the guilt to rest on them...*"[111] The ego's guilt is so acute that it is projected outward onto others; we want others to be the guilty ones so that we feel better about ourselves and so that we won't be punished by God. What we have to remember is that we are still carrying all this guilt around with us to this day.

It seems difficult to understand how we would choose a deadly disease, a life of drudgery or an unhappy marriage, to give a few examples. Surely, we would prefer to make other choices, such as winning the lottery or having perfect health? But Jesus, in *A Course in Miracles*, keeps insisting that we are not victims. *"Deceive yourself no longer that you are helpless in the face of what is done to you...It is impossible the Son of God be merely driven by events outside of him. It is impossible that happenings that come to him were not his choice. His power of decision is the determiner of every situation in which he seems to find himself by chance or accident. No accident nor chance is possible within the universe as God created it, outside of which is nothing...*"[112] No accident nor chance is possible! If we want a better life, it is up to us to change our minds about the meaning of the world.

So, when things are not going our way, we can repeat Lessons 31 and 32 to remind ourselves that we are not victims. Lesson 34, *"I could see peace instead of this,"* is also helpful. It is explained in this lesson that, *"Peace of mind is clearly an internal matter. It must begin with your own thoughts, and then extend outward. It is from your peace of mind that a peaceful perception of the world arises."*

I am not a victim of the world I see because I created it with my thoughts. If I can be kind, loving and forgiving, I will receive kindness, love and forgiveness. It really is that simple but it takes a lot

---

[111] *ACIM*, T587.
[112] *ACIM*, T448.

of trust to come to this realization. It also takes a lot of hard work because every time the ego complains and starts its usual meaningless discussion in our minds, we have to tell it to be quiet and call upon the Holy Spirit for help.

If a relationship comes to an end, it may be tempting to think of oneself as a victim. It is quite a common occurrence for a man (or a woman) to just get up and leave what had been a happy liaison. The rejected partner will wonder what it is they have done wrong, and may take a long time to get over the loss of the love of the other partner. But the Text explains that we should not worry about losing the love of another. Miracles, we are told, make no distinction between one difficulty or another, and are able to heal all of them. Furthermore, *"...In reality you are perfectly unaffected by all expressions of lack of love. These can be from yourself and others, from yourself to others, or from others to you. Peace is an attribute* **in** *you. You cannot find it outside..."* [113]

A useful lesson to use when we feel abandoned or rejected is Lesson 284, *"I can elect to change all thoughts that hurt."* That seems an amazing statement, and when we are in the midst of great suffering it doesn't seem the slightest bit possible. But a closer look at Lesson 284 reveals that, *"Loss is not loss when properly perceived. Pain is impossible. There is no grief with any cause at all. And suffering of any kind is nothing but a dream."* Jesus explains that at first we will repeat this lesson without truly believing in it. Then we will begin to accept it, but not wholeheartedly. Then we will take the lesson seriously and, finally, we will accept it as the truth. Therefore, it may be wise to just repeat this lesson over and over again whenever we are suffering, regardless of the cause.

If we can really accept the idea that we are not victims of our experiences, then it is the beginning of our release from the ego because it means we have started to acknowledge that we have a choice between the ego and the Holy Spirit (which, in fact, is the only choice we have.) As we saw in Chapter 19, if someone expresses anger towards us, it could be that we still have anger within our own minds. Similarly, if we experience someone acting in a selfish way, for

---

[113] *ACIM,* T18.

instance, jumping the queue in front of us, it means we still have traces of selfishness within ourselves. We, therefore, accept this instead of thinking badly about the person who jumped the queue. We forgive him and we ask the Holy Spirit for help once again.

When a crime has been committed both the victim *and* the perpetrator of the crime deserve our sympathy; both are being driven by their deluded egos; both are in need of help and healing. In fact, all of us who have not yet awakened from the dream are in need of help and healing.   The miracle of forgiveness is the remedy, and it is forgiveness which will help us overcome our guilt and ultimately take us Home.

"...Perception is a mirror, not a fact. And what I look on is my state of mind, reflected outward. I would bless the world by looking on it through the eyes of Christ. And I will look upon the certain signs that all my sins have been forgiven me."[114] In other words, by looking upon everything with forgiveness *(through the eyes of Christ)*, we will experience a joyful existence because we will have overcome the guilt in our minds *(signs that all my sins have been forgiven me.)*

We forgive others and we forgive ourselves because we now accept the Atonement. We now accept that we are still in Heaven, at one with God and with all of His creation. This brings us to the realization that the world we live in can only be a dream world or a mental image. So perhaps we can take it less seriously than we have done. And when things get us down, we can remember the message of Lesson 200: *"There is no peace except the peace of God."*

"Seek you no further. You will not find peace except the peace of God. Accept this fact, and save yourself the agony of yet more bitter disappointments, bleak despair, and sense of icy hopelessness and doubt. Seek you no further. There is nothing else for you to find except the peace of God, unless you seek for misery and pain."[115]

If we can forgive and overcome our feelings of having been victimized, we will be able to wipe the slate clean when we meet someone who hurt us in the past. This is what miracles are all about. *"The miracle enables you to see your brother without his past, and so*

---

[114]*ACIM,* W451.

[115] *ACIM,* W384.

perceive him as born again. His errors are all past, and by perceiving him without them you are releasing him. And since his past is yours, you share in this release. "[116]

---

[116] *ACIM,* T251.

CHAPTER 25

FEELING DISSATISFIED AND WANTING
MORE OUT OF LIFE

When we are young there are goals to work towards and things to accomplish that bring fulfillment and a sense of achievement. But the time may come when all the things that previously were fulfilling are no longer so. If this is the case, we may keep on searching for other things in an attempt to find meaning in an ultimately meaningless world. This could lead us to change our jobs, our homes, our partners or our lifestyle. We may suddenly pack everything in and go on a trip around the world. Or we may aim for a better position at work in the hope of making more money. If we succeed at this, we may buy a second or third home, more cars, jewelry, clothes, etc. But, if we are wise we will, at some point in our lives, stop and ask ourselves this very pertinent question: "How can illusions satisfy us?"

"How can illusions satisfy God's Son," is Lesson 272 in the Workbook. In this lesson we read, *"Today we pass illusions by. And if we hear temptation call to us to stay and linger in a dream, we turn aside and ask ourselves if we, the Sons of God, could be content with dreams, when Heaven can be chosen just as easily as hell, and love will happily replace all fear."*[117] It is, of course, the fear of going without that makes us search for more and more in our lives. The fear of being hungry drives us to work our way up the career ladder. The fear of being lonely motivates us to find a partner. The fear of ageing induces us to try to hold back the hands of time. All these are valid ego fears but this doesn't make them real. The ego's belief system is based on lack. So it searches for ways to compensate for this. We see this not only in individuals but also in nations. As mentioned before, some nations wage wars over land belonging to their neighbors. Others wage wars over the scarce resources of water and oil. This can only lead to strife; it will never lead to peace because, *"There is no peace, except*

---

[117] *ACIM,* W432.

the peace of God. "[118]

Lesson 76, *"I am under no laws but God's,"* asks us, quite bluntly, to change our minds about all the things that we believe are meaningful. Jesus tells us that the laws of God can never be replaced by any of our made-up laws, such as, *"...the 'laws' of nutrition, of immunization, of medication, and of the body's protection in innumerable ways. Think further; you believe in the 'laws' of friendship, of 'good' relationships and reciprocity. Perhaps you even think that there are laws which set forth what is God's and what is yours. Many 'religions' have been based on this. They would not save but damn in Heaven's name...There are no laws but God's. Dismiss all foolish magical beliefs today, and hold your mind in silent readiness to hear the Voice that speaks the truth to you."* [119] There is a very good reason why our beliefs about this world and our laws should be dismissed: they are made up. *"...There is no world apart from your ideas because ideas leave not their source, and you maintain the world within your mind in thought."* [120]

The things we think we need in our lives are referred to as *"idols"* by the Course. We think they will bring us happiness but, even if they do, they could keep us from awakening and finding our way back Home, unless we are very vigilant. The ego's purpose of idols is exactly that—to keep us trapped in the illusion instead of becoming healed and aware that we are still as we were when God created us. *"...To seek a special person or a thing to add to you to make yourself complete, can only mean that you believe some form is missing. And by finding this, you will achieve completion in a form you like. This is the purpose of an idol; that you will not look beyond it, to the source of the belief that you are incomplete..."* [121] If we are honest with ourselves we will acknowledge that we search for the perfect partner, the perfect job or house or car or piece of jewelry to make us feel better about ourselves. But we have no need to find external things to boost our worth because we are all holy Sons of God, whole and complete as we

---

[118] *ACIM*, W384.
[119] *ACIM*, W135.
[120] *ACIM*, W243.
[121] *ACIM*, T631.

were when He created us.

It's precisely because we fail to recognize that there is nothing worthwhile in this world, that we are not motivated to awaken. *"Who would be willing to be turned away from all the roadways of the world, unless he understood their real futility? Is it not needful that he should begin with this, to seek another way instead? For while he sees a choice where there is none, what power of decision can he use?"*[122] Recognizing that we don't have any real choices in this world is very important. It *appears* that we do have many choices but *all the choices we make are within the illusion*, i.e., we are simply replacing one illusory thing with another, which is pointless. *"There is no choice where every end is sure. Perhaps you would prefer to try them all, before you really learn they are but one. The roads this world can offer seem to be quite large in number, but the time must come when everyone begins to see how like they are to one another....All must reach this point and go beyond it..."*[123] Those who are searching for meaning, such as students of *A Course in Miracles*, have reached this point and have decided to *"go beyond it."*

When we notice we are continually searching for one thing after another to bring meaning to our lives we can affirm to ourselves: *"I will not value what is valueless."* Lesson 133 reminds us, *"There are no satisfactions in the world,"* and it states that if we choose something that is temporary, then it has no value; if we choose something that belongs to someone else, then it has no value; and if what we desire makes us feel guilty, then it is definitely an ego goal and, therefore, has no value. *"Heaven itself is reached with empty hands and open minds, which come with nothing to find everything and claim it as their own."*[124] In other words, we can reach Heaven without any of the things we think we need here on earth. But we do need to have an open mind. It is probably true to say that the students of *A Course in Miracles* have open minds because they are trying, with the help of the Course, to change their perception of the world. When we reach Heaven we arrive with nothing but we find everything—

---

[122] *ACIM,* T654.

[123] *ACIM,* T653.

[124] *ACIM,* W247.

that's a most encouraging thought.

All of us on this planet believe this world has something to offer; if we didn't believe this, we wouldn't be here. We would have already ascended and given up on this world. This is explained clearly in the following passage: *"No one who comes here but must still have some hope, some lingering illusion, or some dream that there is something outside of himself that will bring happiness and peace to him. If everything is in him this cannot be so. And therefore by his coming, he denies the truth about himself, and seeks for something more than everything, as if a part of it were separated off and found where all the rest of it is not..."*[125] The problem is that if we continue searching for idols within the illusion we will remain trapped. *"The lingering illusion will impel him to seek out a thousand idols, and to seek beyond them for a thousand more. And each will fail him, all excepting one; for he will die, and does not understand the idol that he seeks **is** but his death..."*

It might help if we look back and take stock of our lives. Are there any repeating patterns? Are there things that we seem to keep doing in our lives that aren't really very helpful to our growth as spiritual beings? Then we can ask ourselves if there any changes we could make which would speed us on our journey Home. If we are happy to keep going the way we always have done in the past, maybe we aren't quite ready yet to relinquish the ego. That should not cause us too much concern because the time *will* come when we are ready. In the meantime, we could help ourselves by asking, *"How can illusions satisfy God's Son?"* Eventually, it will become apparent that illusions can't satisfy us.

---

[125] *ACIM,* T617.

CHAPTER 26

FEELING THE NEED TO DEFEND ONESELF

We all feel the need to defend ourselves; this is a common human reaction to criticism, which we deem to be unfair, or to a perceived threat of some sort. But students of *A Course in Miracles* are well aware that they should not defend themselves because, in doing so, they are making the illusions of the world real. Remember, if someone says something unpleasant, they are only figures in a dream world, so why react to them?

"Forget not, when you feel the need arise to be defensive about anything, you have identified yourself with an illusion. And therefore feel that you are weak because you are alone..."[126] If we don't want to identify with illusions we need to resist the temptation to stand up for ourselves when we are criticized about something or misjudged or accused of something we haven't done. It can be very difficult to resist this temptation but when we are able to just shrug our shoulders and walk away without feeling the need to defend ourselves, we will have made very good progress as a Course student. It means that we have finally realized that nothing is worth defending in this world. It also shows that we are able to forgive and forget. But, obviously, if we are accused of a crime we didn't commit we will have to defend ourselves and prove our innocence *within the dream.*

"Who would defend himself unless he thought he were attacked, that the attack were real, and that his own defense could save himself? And herein lies the folly of defense; it gives illusions full reality, and then attempts to handle them as real. It adds illusions to illusions, thus making correction doubly difficult. And it is this you do when you attempt to plan the future, activate the past, or organize the present as you wish."[127] This is what we read in Lesson 135, *"If I defend myself I am attacked."* And this is a useful lesson to recall whenever we are

---

[126] *ACIM*, T480.
[127] *ACIM*, W252.

on the verge of defending ourselves.

In Chapter 30 of the Text, Jesus draws an analogy between our "idols" (i.e., practically everything in the physical world) and children's toys. He points out that a child may be frightened by a toy that squeaks but when he grows up he realizes there was nothing to fear. Similarly, our "toys" must be discarded and not grieved for because they never brought us joy. *"But neither were they things to frighten you, nor make you safe if they obeyed your rules. They must be neither cherished nor attacked, but merely looked upon as children's toys without a single meaning of their own....God's Son needs no defense against his dreams. His idols do not threaten him at all. His one mistake is that he thinks them real. What can the power of illusions do?"*[128] This implies that all the things we believe will keep us safe, such as money, medicine and locked doors, are just illusions that do not need defending. But it takes a huge amount of trust to accept this.

We all make plans for the future in an attempt to find safety and comfort as we grow older. Yet even plans are idols, according to Jesus, because they are attempts to rely on the body to protect us when, in fact, only the truth will do so. *"The mind engaged in planning for itself is occupied in setting up control of future happenings. It does not think that it will be provided for, unless it makes its own provisions....Defenses are the plans you undertake to make against the truth."* Then he asks us to trust God, *"What could you not accept, if you but knew that everything that happens, all events, past, present and to come, are gently planned by One Whose only purpose is your good?...Your present trust in Him is the defense that promises a future undisturbed, without a trace of sorrow, and with joy that constantly increases, as this life becomes a holy instant, set in time, but heeding only immortality..."*[129]

We defend ourselves because we feel threatened; and we feel threatened because we feel weak; we feel weak because we identify solely with our physical bodies (and they *are* weak.) So we defend ourselves when someone accuses us of something, and we defend our

---

[128] *ACIM*, T634.
[129] *ACIM*, W255.

nation when another nation attacks us. *A Course in Miracles* is not telling us not to defend ourselves if we are attacked physically in the streets, for example; neither is it telling us not to defend our country. Obviously, if we are attacked physically we have to do whatever we can to protect ourselves. But what it is saying is that we need to transfer our identification from our bodies to our minds. We need to become right-minded and follow the guidance of the Holy Spirit. Lesson 201 could be used to help one identify a little less with the body: *"I am not a body. I am free. For I am still as God created me."*

The difficulty lies in the fact that we don't recognize that it is the mind that governs the body. The body itself is just a neutral thing, as we read in Lesson 294: *"My body is a wholly neutral thing"*. In this lesson we are reminded that, *"Its neutrality protects it while it has a use."* Being neutral, the body is incapable of maintaining itself in a healthy condition or of defending itself. If we can keep our thoughts positive and strong and remember that we are holy Sons of God, it is unlikely that harm will befall our physical form. If we focus on possible fearful events (e.g. serious ill health, crime, accidents, etc.) we will *attract these things* into our lives. It, therefore, makes sense to be very vigilant about what one allows into one's mind. We need to switch off the radio, for instance, when a particular disease is discussed. There are frequent advertisements both on the radio and television which encourage people to make claims for personal injury if they have been the victim of an accident that was not their fault. Well, the more one listens to this sort of thing, the more likely one is to suffer an accident because the mind rules the body. This is basic common sense but, sadly, people don't realize the damage that comes from listening to negative news bulletins, advertisements or the accounts of friends and family members of the mishaps that have befallen them. Obviously, one has to offer a comforting ear to those in trouble but one needs to try to detach from the drama nonetheless.

Similarly, the more we listen to accounts of a financial collapse or economic recession, the more likely we are to have a recession; and the more we discuss all the other woes of the planet, the more likely we are to create them. We attract what we focus on and what we fear. The solution is to try to develop a positive outlook and to focus on what we want to have in our lives.

A useful lesson to use when we feel we should defend ourselves is Lesson 153, *"In my defenselessness my safety lies."* This lesson, referred to previously in Chapter 5, starts off with this stark warning, *"You who feel threatened by this changing world, its twists of fortune and its bitter jests, its brief relationships and all the 'gifts' it merely lends to take away again; attend this lesson well. The world provides no safety. It is rooted in attack, and all its 'gifts' of seeming safety are illusory deceptions. It attacks, and then attacks again. No peace of mind is possible where danger threatens thus..."*[130] There is surely nobody on earth who hasn't experienced the *"twists of fortune"* mentioned above. But, in Lesson 153, Jesus gives us yet another reason why we should not defend ourselves. *"Defenselessness is strength. It testifies to recognition of the Christ in you...Defensiveness is weakness. It proclaims you have denied the Christ and come to fear His Father's anger..."* And then he has these encouraging words for us, *"We look past dreams today, and recognize that we need no defense because we are created unassailable, without all thought or wish or dream in which attack has any meaning."*[131]

The Course tells us that the body is merely a *"little pile of dust and water"* that our (ego) minds believe must be protected. But we must constantly remember the neutrality of the body and the power that the mind has over it, as mentioned earlier on in this chapter. *"The body is in need of no defense. This cannot be too often emphasized. It will be strong and healthy if the mind does not abuse it by assigning it to roles it cannot fill, to purposes beyond its scope, and to exalted aims which it cannot accomplish."*[132]

It is heartening to realize that the body will be strong and healthy when it serves the Holy Spirit. How does it do that? Throughout the Course we are told the only function of the body is communication. It is a neutral thing that can be put to serve God's plan, if it is used to communicate with others and help others awaken from the dream and, above all, if it is used to forgive others. But if it is used merely as a tool of the ego, to serve its own separate interests and reinforce the

---

[130] *ACIM*, W284.
[131] *ACIM*, W285.
[132] *ACIM*, W253.

idea of the separation from God, then it is not fulfilling its divine function and it will appear in need of defense.

As we read in the Workbook, *"The body is a fence the Son of God imagines he has built, to separate parts of his Self from other parts. It is within this fence he thinks he lives, to die as it decays and crumbles."*[133] However, it is not all gloom and doom because we can actually use the illusory body to awaken from the dream. "*....But we can change the purpose that the body will obey by changing what we think that it is for. The body is the means by which God's Son returns to sanity. Though it was made to fence him into hell without escape, yet has the goal of Heaven been exchanged for the pursuit of hell. The Son of God extends his hand to reach his brother, and to help him walk along the road with him. Now is the body holy. Now it serves to heal the mind that it was made to kill."*

We are told that when the body becomes holy by serving Jesus or the Holy Spirit, and it reaches out to help others, we will not have to worry about its safety, and so we will not feel the need to defend ourselves. We will also no longer feel the need to, *"...attempt to plan the future, activate the past, or organize the present..."* We will simply trust that we are being guided.

But *how* are we guided by the Holy Spirit? Some people are fortunate enough to actually hear His Voice in their heads. But that is not the only way to receive His guidance. He could speak to us in our dreams at night, through our gut feelings or when we get flashes of inspiration, which make us feel compelled to take action. By being guided in this way, we tend to plan less and not worry so much about the future. We move from fear-based actions to love and trust. We become more Self-reliant as opposed to self-reliant, where the self is the portion of the mind that listens to the ego. Whilst it is human nature to make plans for the future, and it is something we all do, the more we trust in God and in His guidance, the easier it becomes not to plan so much; we can now sit back a little and see where life takes us.

---

[133] *ACIM,* W425.

CHAPTER 27

UPLIFTING LESSONS TO LIGHT THE WAY

And now for something positive—lessons we can use to focus our minds and speed us on our journey Home.

There are so many Workbook lessons we can use to raise our spirits and give us hope and meaning whilst we appear to be living in this world. These lessons also teach us how to coexist harmoniously with the rest of mankind and, better still, teach us how to help others whilst helping ourselves. It is important to use these inspiring lessons because there will be times in our lives when we feel sad and disillusioned about the world we are living in. It is difficult at times being a Course student knowing that everything around us is unreal, and yet not knowing exactly how or when we will awaken from our dream world. As Jesus tells us in the Course, *"This world you seem to live in is not home to you. And somewhere in your mind you know that this is true. A memory of home keeps haunting you, as if there were a place that called you to return, although you do not recognize the voice, nor what it is the voice reminds you of. Yet still you feel an alien here, from somewhere all unknown..."*[134] It is, consequently, not surprising that we feel sad or lost at times. The simple reason is that we are not at home here on earth, and we have a vague recollection of our true home although we are not conscious of this. There are two ways of overcoming this problem. We can either pretend this is our home, and find countless things to do to distract us from our innate sadness, or we can find a path that will lead us to our true Home.

"I am surrounded by the Love of God,"[135] is a wonderful lesson to start with as it is very reassuring. Lesson 264 reminds us that God is always with us: *"Father, You stand before me and behind, beside me, in the place I see myself, and everywhere I go. You are in all the things I look upon, the sounds I hear, and every hand that reaches for* my

---

[134] *ACIM*, W339.
[135] *ACIM*, W427.

own. In You time disappears, and place becomes a meaningless belief..." Lesson 264 is also empowering because it reminds us of our divine inner strength: *"Father, Your Son is like Yourself..."*

Lesson 131, *"No one can fail who seeks to reach the truth,"* has to be one of the most encouraging and motivating lessons of *A Course in Miracles.* This lesson points out that we are searching for things but do not realize that we are actually searching for Heaven. *"You look for permanence in the impermanent, for love where there is none, for safety in the midst of danger; immortality within the darkness of the dream of death...Be glad that search you must. Be glad as well to learn you search for Heaven, and must find the goal you really want. No one can fail to want this goal and reach it in the end."*[136] The last sentence of that passage should be re-read. The good thing about Lesson 131 is that it offers us hope. We *cannot fail* in our spiritual quest. We *can* succeed in our quest for immortality, if we follow the advice given to us. We are asked to watch all our thoughts and let them go, and then beneath them is a door which will lead us from illusion to truth. We are guided by the Holy Spirit, who walks with us, and we should be happy because: *"This is a day of gladness, for we come to the appointed time and place where you will find the goal of all your searching here, and all the seeking of the world, which end together as you pass beyond the door."*

In Chapter 13 of the Text, we are given further reassurance that the Holy Spirit will help lead us Home. *"Fear not the Holy Spirit will fail in what your Father has given Him to do. The Will of God can fail in nothing. Have faith in only this one thing, and it will be sufficient: God wills you be in Heaven, and nothing can keep you from it, or it from you."*[137] We can't fail to reach the truth because God has given us the Holy Spirit to show us the Way. But what we have to do is to welcome Him into our lives and remember to call upon Him regularly.

There may be times when we need to remind ourselves that *"There is one life, and that I share with God."*[138] Lesson 167 will reinforce in our minds the fact that the only form of life that is real is the life we

---

[136] *ACIM,* W239.

[137] *ACIM,* T268.

[138] *ACIM,* W318.

share with God, and everything in our ego-manufactured world is an illusion; it follows that death is an illusion too. *"There are not different kinds of life, for life is like the truth. It does not have degrees. It is the one condition in which all that God created share. Like all His Thoughts, it has no opposite. There is no death because what God created shares His life. There is no death because an opposite to God does not exist. There is no death because the Father and the Son are one."*

"Your grace is given me. I claim it now," states Lesson 168. This is a most inspiring lesson which teaches us that, by the grace of God, we can awaken and become liberated. It offers hope in a world of despair; it offers us joy as it shows us a way out of the trap set up by the ego. Grace, this wonderful gift of God, will help us awaken from the dream. God gives us this gift because He loves us. We may not know exactly how much He does love us; but if we knew, we would become joyous and carefree. *"If you but knew the meaning of His Love, hope and despair would be impossible. For hope would be forever satisfied; despair of any kind unthinkable..."*[139]

Lesson 169, *"By grace I live. By grace I am released,"* explains the importance of grace—it will lead us to the truth. *"Grace is an aspect of the Love of God which is most like the state prevailing in the unity of truth. It is the world's most lofty aspiration, for it leads beyond the world entirely..."*[140] This lesson also deals with our innate oneness with each other and with God. The following quotation, mentioned previously, is an important one: *"Oneness is simply the idea God is. And in His Being, He encompasses all things..."* Just remembering those two key words, *"God is,"* can put a smile on one's face.

Another lesson which can also make us smile is Lesson 320, *"My Father gives all power unto me."* This empowering lesson reminds us of our true strength, which is based on the strength of God. Because we are one with Him we share His strength with Him. *"The Son of God is limitless. There are no limits on his strength, his peace, his joy, nor any attributes his Father gave in his creation...I am he in whom*

---

[139] *ACIM,* W321.
[140] *ACIM,* W323.

the power of my Father's Will abides."[141]

"The light of the world brings peace to every mind through my forgiveness." Do we realize that we can actually bring peace to every mind? Lesson 63 is saying exactly that. *"How holy are you who have the power to bring peace to every mind! How blessed are you who can learn to recognize the means for letting this be done through you!"[142]* The means for bringing peace is, of course, forgiveness. Forgiveness transforms us from being an ego-based individual living in a dream world into a powerful, spiritual being who can light the world with the light of Christ. *"You are indeed the light of the world with such a function."* Lesson 63 continues in the same positive way, as it asks us to repeat the following throughout the day, *"The light of the world brings peace to every mind through my forgiveness. I am the means God has appointed for the salvation of the world."*

In Chapter 17 of the text it is explained that forgiveness will lead us across a little bridge that takes us out of our illusory world into the *"real world,"* in which everything shines brightly because everything has been forgiven. *"This little step, so small it has escaped your notice, is a stride through time into eternity, beyond all ugliness into beauty that will enchant you, and will never cease to cause you wonderment at its perfection."[143]*

In Lesson 195, *"Love is the Way I walk in gratitude,"* we are told that the reason to be grateful is that we have not separated from God. Therefore, we are all as whole and as immortal as He is. *"We thank our Father for one thing alone; that we are separate from no living thing, and therefore one with Him."[144]* It is important to cultivate gratitude because gratitude is, *"the way of love."* Lesson 195 makes another very significant point: we also need to be grateful for the fact that we are one with the rest of humanity, and in helping others to awaken to the truth we are, in fact, helping ourselves too. *"Then let our brothers lean their tired heads against our shoulders as they rest a while. We offer thanks for them. For if we can direct them to the peace*

---

[141] *ACIM*, W460.

[142] *ACIM*, W105.

[143] *ACIM*, T353.

[144] *ACIM*, W373.

that we would find, the way is opening at last to us."

Lesson 127, *"There is no love but God's,"* is another wonderful lesson. It ends with a lovely blessing, which could be used every day. We simply need to mentally greet everyone we come across—friends, colleagues and passersby—with the following: *"I bless you, brother, with the Love of God, which I would share with you."*[145] (This is a shortened version of the one given in Lesson 127.)

One final lesson to end this book and one of the most uplifting of all is Lesson 156, *"I walk with God in perfect holiness."* This lesson should wipe away all guilt and fear. If we walk with God in perfect holiness it means that we are not guilty of having separated from Him; we are not weak, vulnerable and at the mercy of the ego; we are whole and complete and in the company of God, even though it may not be apparent to us. The last few lines of Lesson 156 summarize the key teachings of *A Course in Miracles* in a beautiful way: *"I walk with God in perfect holiness. I light the world, I light my mind and all the minds which God created one with me."*

There is One God, One Life and One Mind, and we are all part of this Oneness.

---

[145] *ACIM,* W232.

APPENDIX

Annoyance related to the past.

Lesson 8: My mind is preoccupied with past thoughts.

Lesson 289: The past is over. It can touch me not.

Seeing conflict on the TV news.

Lesson 12: I am upset because I see a meaningless world.

Lesson 14: God did not create a meaningless world.

Lesson 21: I am determined to see things differently.

Lesson 23: I can escape from the world I see by giving up attack thoughts.

Lesson 34: I could see peace instead of this.

Feeling anger towards someone or something.

Lesson 22: What I see is a form of vengeance.

Lesson 23: I can escape from the world I see by giving up attack thoughts.

Lesson 68: Love holds no grievances.

Feeling agitated, troubled and anxious

Lesson 48: There is nothing to fear.

Lesson 74: There is no will but God's.

Lesson 193: All things are lessons God would have me learn.

Feeling weak and vulnerable.

Lesson 47: God is the strength in which I trust.

Lesson 26: My attack thoughts are attacking my invulnerability.

Lesson 153: In my defenselessness my safety lies.

Lesson 41: God goes with me wherever I go.

Feeling resentful or unforgiving.

Lesson 73: I will there be light.

Lesson 75: The light has come.

Feeling lost and wanting to discover your divine purpose

Lesson 98: I will accept my part in God's plan for salvation.

Lesson 192: I have a function God would have me fill.

Lesson 99: Salvation is my only function here.

Worrying about ill health and experiencing pain.

Lessons 210 & 215: I am not a body, I am free. For I am still as God created me.

Lesson 140: Only salvation can be said to cure.

Being afraid of death.

Lesson 163: There is no death. The Son of God is free.

Lesson 167: There is one life, and that I share with God.

Lesson 95: I am one Self, united with my Creator.

Feeling mistrustful about someone.

Lesson 181: I trust my brothers, who are one with me.

Lesson 351: My sinless brother is my guide to peace. My sinful brother is my guide to pain. And which I choose to see I will behold.

Unable to meditate and calm the mind.

Lesson 106: Let me be still and listen to the truth.

Lesson 221: Peace to my mind. Let all my thoughts be still.

Lesson 291: This is a day of stillness and of peace.

Lesson 49: God's Voice speaks to me all through the day.

Worrying about the future.

Lesson 194: I place the future in the Hands of God.

Lesson 76: I am under no laws but God's.

Lesson 47: God is the strength in which I trust.

Lesson 292: A happy outcome to all things is sure.

Feeling trapped in the world of the ego.

Lesson 23: I can escape from the world I see by giving up attack thoughts.

Lesson 49: God's Voice speaks to me all through the day.

Lesson 182: I will be still an instant and go home.

Lesson 226: My home awaits me. I will hasten there.

Lesson 327: I need but call and You will answer me.

Feeling unhappy, anxious or afraid due to difficult circumstances.

Lesson 193: All things are lessons God would have me learn.

Lesson 12: I am upset because I see a meaningless world.

Lesson 11: My meaningless thoughts are showing me a meaningless world.

Lesson 248: What suffers is not part of me.

Lesson 327: I need but call and You will answer me.

Lesson 361: This holy instant would I give to You. Be You in charge for I would follow You, certain that Your direction gives me peace.

When things no longer appeal to you.

Lesson 128: The world I see holds nothing that I want.

Lesson 129: Beyond this world there is a world I want.

Lesson 224: God is my Father, and He loves His Son.

Lesson 272: How can illusions satisfy God's Son?

Having low self-esteem and a lack of self-confidence

Lesson 35: My mind is part of God's. I am very holy.

Lesson 299: Eternal holiness abides in me.

Lesson 186: Salvation of the world depends on me.

Feeling frightened about what lies ahead

Lesson 240: Fear is not justified in any form.

Lesson 244: I am in danger nowhere in the world.

Lesson 337: My sinlessness protects me from all harm.

Lesson 193: All things are lessons God would have me learn.

Lesson 46: God is the Love in which I forgive.

Being too distracted by daily activities to think of God

Lesson 64: Let me not forget my function.

Lesson 232: Be in my mind, my Father, through the day.

Lesson 231: Father, I will but to remember You.

Lesson 258: Let me remember that my goal is God.

Lesson 221: Peace to my mind. Let all my thoughts be still.

Lesson 125: In quiet I receive God's Word today.

Lesson 185: I want the peace of God.

Lesson 254: Let every voice but God's be still in me.

Judging someone who has done something wrong.

Lesson 259: Let me remember that there is no sin.

Lesson 335: I choose to see my brother's sinlessness.

Lesson 243: Today I will judge nothing that occurs.

Lesson 266: My holy Self abides in you, God's Son.

Lesson 288: Let me forget my brother's past today.

Lesson 352: Judgment and love are opposites.

Feeling different from others.

Lesson 164: Now are we one with Him Who is our Source.

Lesson 181: I trust my brothers, who are one with me.

Lesson 243: Today I will judge nothing that occurs.

Lesson 95: I am one Self, united with my Creator.

When responding to a difficult person or situation.

Lesson 193: All things are lessons God would have me learn.

Lesson 23: I can escape from the world I see by giving up attack thoughts.

Lesson 243: Today I will judge nothing that occurs.

Lesson 333: Forgiveness ends the dream of conflict here.

Lesson 107: Truth will correct all errors in my mind.

Lesson 232: Be in my mind, my Father, through the day.

Feeling guilty.

Lesson 35: My mind is part of God's. I am very holy.

Lesson 190: I choose the joy of God instead of pain.

Lesson 156: I walk with God in perfect holiness.

Feeling sad and upset because of all the cruelty in the world.

Lesson 14: God did not create a meaningless world.

Lesson 12: I am upset because I see a meaningless world.

Lesson 23: I can escape from the world I see by giving up attack thoughts.

Lesson 301: And God Himself shall wipe away all tears.

Lesson 63: The light of the world brings peace to every mind through my forgiveness.

Feeling unfairly treated by someone or by circumstances.

Lesson 31: I am not the victim of the world I see.

Lesson 32: I have invented the world I see.

Lesson 34: I could see peace instead of this.

Lesson 284: I can elect to change all thoughts that hurt.

Lesson 200: There is no peace except the peace of God.

Feeling dissatisfied and wanting more out of life.

Lesson 272: How can illusions satisfy God's Son?

Lesson 200: There is no peace except the peace of God

Lesson 76: I am under no laws but God's.

Lesson 133: I will not value what is valueless.

Feeling the need to defend oneself

Lesson 135: If I defend myself I am attacked.

Lesson 201: I am not a body. I am free. For I am still as God created
me.

Lesson 294: My body is a wholly neutral thing.

Lesson 153: In my defenselessness my safety lies.

Uplifting Lessons to light the Way

Lesson 264: I am surrounded by the Love of God.

Lesson 131: No one can fail who seeks to reach the truth.

Lesson 167: There is one life, and that I share with God.

Lesson 168: Your grace is given me. I claim it now.

Lesson 169: By grace I live. By grace I am released.

Lesson 320: My Father gives all power unto me.

Lesson 63: The light of the world brings peace to every mind through
my forgiveness.

Lesson 195: Love is the Way I walk in gratitude.

Lesson 127: There is no love but God's.

Lesson 156: I walk with God in perfect holiness.

About the Author

Raveena Nash has been a student of *A Course in Miracles* for several years. As soon as she discovered this great spiritual teaching, she felt drawn to it and realized that this was her Path.

The central teaching of *ACIM* is that the ego, the physical body and the world of time and space are illusions. God created the spirit not the human body; therefore, only the spirit is real. *ACIM* is the Path of Forgiveness as it shows how forgiveness will heal our minds and help us awaken from the dream of life on earth.

In her first book, *It's All An Illusion!*, Raveena compared the belief system of *ACIM* with other spiritual paths. In *Rise Above*, she offers practical advice and guidance to help the spiritual seeker make progress along the Path of Forgiveness. She shows how certain *A Course in Miracles* Workbook Lessons can be used to overcome a variety of problems in our everyday lives.

Raveena has a London University Honors degree in economics. She has worked as a mathematics and special needs teacher and a radio and television newsreader. She has also written articles for a weekly newspaper. She is interested in holistic healing and is a trained Reiki and Reconnective Healing practitioner. She now lives in rural England with her two cats. Her interests include reading, classical music, going for walks in the countryside, growing fruit and vegetables and baking cakes. Her main concern now is to awaken from the dream or the illusion in which we are all immersed, and to help others to awaken too.

**Raveena Nash welcomes contact about her book
and related topics by email to:**
allanillusion@live.com

www.ingramcontent.com/pod-product-compliance
Lightning Source LLC
Chambersburg PA
CBHW021834020426
42334CB00014B/625